When School Policies Backfire

When School Policies Backfire

How Well-Intended Measures
Can Harm Our Most
Vulnerable Students

Michael A. Gottfried
Gilberto Q. Conchas

Editors

Harvard Education Press
Cambridge, Massachusetts

Library of Congress Control Number 2015953168

Paperback ISBN 978-1-61250-907-5
Library Edition ISBN 978-1-61250-908-2

Published by Harvard Education Press,
an imprint of the Harvard Education Publishing Group

Harvard Education Press
8 Story Street
Cambridge, MA 02138

Cover Design: Saizon Design
Cover Photo: Monkey Business Images/Shutterstock.com
The typefaces used in this book are DIN, Futura, Helvetica Neue, and Minion

CONTENTS

FOREWORD

What happens when well-intended educational policies go wrong, really wrong, exacerbating the very problems they were aiming to solve? This is a compelling issue that demands attention, yet has been understudied. While much has been written on the unintended consequences of policies, policy backfire has received little attention in the field of education. This volume fills this important niche. Michael Gottfried and Gilberto Conchas bring together an esteemed group of authors to share six detailed, critical case studies of policy backfire in education. The chapters in this volume provide vital lessons that can help avoid some of the damaging consequences of policy backfire in the future.

Several of the chapters address issues arising from the local responses to No Child Left Behind. Under pressure to respond to state and national accountability systems, well-meaning local educators make critical educational decisions using data. Sometimes these decisions are misinformed, despite the best intentions. Data-driven decision making has become widespread in the past decade, and educators are expected to use data such as test scores and dropout rates to drive decisions. At the same time, many principals and teachers feel ill-equipped to make informed decisions on the basis of data, in large part because they have not had sufficient training or because they lack time. Educators often find themselves making quick decisions with limited information because they are forced to show they are "doing something" in response to the data. This is a key moment when policy backfire can occur. Data tend to be used as part of a triage process that focuses on the most "needy" students, rather than an inquiry-oriented process of continuous improvement that benefits all students.

Chapters in this volume also address the backfire that occurs with locally developed policies, not just that arising from state or national policies. This is important, as indeed many policies originate at the local level and in theory such policies should be more attentive to the school context than those developed farther away. However, this is not always the case, as the examples in the book make clear. Local decisions regarding school closure, school choice, and a one-to-one computer program did not account for the ways in which these policies would play out for students, families, and/or teachers. The experiences and belief systems of these key stakeholders were not considered as part of the policy process, and the consequence was policy backfire.

The most troubling aspect of the policy backfire examples shared in this book is the negative effect on the education of underserved students. Already marginalized in US education systems, low-income students and students of color disproportionately experience further setbacks as a result of various policies. Instead of experiencing expanded learning opportunities, these students face more limited prospects. While recent accountability policies and the use of data have brought attention to the academic performance of student subgroups, the ways in which educators at the local level have responded to these data have not always been beneficial. For example, many schools and districts offer intervention programs for students identified as struggling. While these interventions have laudable goals, their implementation does not always match up to the ideal, and in some cases it backfires, as this book points out.

This book should be essential reading for anyone involved in establishing educational policies, including at the local level. Its lessons are important not only for government policy makers, school board members, and district and school leaders, but also for the teacher making classroom-, grade-, or department-level decisions. These microlevel decisions have long-term consequences for children's learning. Take the following case in point: A team of teachers in an elementary school has developed their own policy regarding math instruction. They assess all students at the beginning of the year to determine which students will get placed into an advanced-level math class. They administer three assessments and determine the cutoff scores by which students will or will not qualify. While aiming to target instruction to the students' individual needs and drawing on multiple forms of data, this policy does not account for the negative effects for the students placed in the "regular" class, including lower self-efficacy in math and less rigorous math instruction. The effects for these students are long lasting, having an impact well beyond elementary school.

Apart from ensuring that this book gets into the hands of key individuals across the educational system, how might we convey its important lessons to the right people? One possibility is to pose several core questions during the policy development process. These might include:

- How does this policy help to improve the educational experience of *all* students?
- Are we keeping the goal of equity front and center?
- How are we meaningfully incorporating the input of students, teachers, and community members into the policy process?
- Have we been honest with these stakeholders and ourselves about the potential short- and long-term effects?
- Are there any perverse incentives involved with this policy?
- Are we taking sufficient time to carefully examine a wide range of data and explore all possible options and outcomes as we work toward policy development?

While thoughtfully addressing these questions may not avoid all cases of policy backfire, it will hopefully inspire dialogue around key issues. However, much of what we know about the policy development and implementation process runs counter to deep inquiry around these kinds of questions. For this reason, we also need community involvement. Parents, students, and community organizations also need to be aware of the lessons in this book so that they can help pose some of these questions and advocate for policies that are in the best interests of all students.

—Amanda Datnow
Professor of Education Studies
Associate Dean, Division of Social Sciences
University of California, San Diego

When Good Policies Go Bad

Michael A. Gottfried, Gilberto Q. Conchas,
Cameron Sublett, and Odelia Simon

It was a searing reminder of the harms of recreational drug use. Indeed, few commercials in history are as memorable as the 1987 *This Is Your Brain on Drugs* public service announcement produced by what was then the Partnership for a Drug-Free America. The message was clear: "This is your brain," the nice man said, as he held up for the camera an unsullied, white egg. The camera then panned to a black, cast-iron skillet perched on the stovetop. "This is drugs," he said, pointing to the skillet. And then, with one crack on the rim, the man dropped the egg into the sizzling, hot skillet. As the egg fried and withered, the man lifted the skillet to the camera and said, "This is your brain on drugs. Any questions?"

This Is Your Brain on Drugs is revered by marketing experts as one of the most influential advertisements of all time. And from a marketing perspective, it is easy to see why. The elements within the ad were simple—a man, an egg, and a hot skillet—and yet the message was profound and lasting. But it is important to consider the ad from another perspective, a policy perspective. From this perspective, the question is not "was the ad good?" but instead "did the ad work?" In other words, was the commercial effective? And more broadly, did the strict, "just say no," antidrug policies of the late 1980s and 1990s, of which ads like *This Is Your Brain on Drugs* were one small component, actually deter children from using drugs? It turns out to be a complicated question. Let's examine why.

Around the same time that the Partnership for a Drug-Free America was orchestrating its campaign to combat the growing narcotics problem facing the nation, individuals from the Los Angeles Police Department and the Los Angeles Unified School District began developing what later became the Drug Abuse Resistance Education (D.A.R.E.) program. Project D.A.R.E. is America's largest school-based drug use prevention program.[1] At its peak, D.A.R.E. had an annual budget of three quarters of a billion dollars. Students at 75 percent of the nation's schools participated in D.A.R.E. activities.[2] In the mid 1990s and even up until recently, D.A.R.E. was everywhere: television ads, bumper stickers, hats, billboards, and even collectible matchbox cars (which you can still buy on eBay!). However, today project D.A.R.E. is likely best remembered among children of the 1990s for its iconic T-shirts, which they wore proudly as kids but now wear ironically. But why all the hip irreverence?

Well, by most measures project D.A.R.E. has been a costly failure. According to one meta-analysis of the many effectiveness evaluations of the program, D.A.R.E.'s short-term ability to reduce or prevent drug use was "small."[3] The same results apply to many of the longitudinal analyses of D.A.R.E.—there simply is little scientific evidence to suggest that students who participated in project D.A.R.E. were less likely to use drugs and tobacco than students who did not.[4] But not only does it appear clear that project D.A.R.E. failed, even worse, some studies have found that students who participated in D.A.R.E. were actually *more likely* to experiment with drugs after D.A.R.E. education.[5] This suggests that project D.A.R.E. may have backfired. Perhaps by informing children of the various drugs that exist, D.A.R.E. actually made children more likely to seek out and try those drugs! In other words, telling children to "just say no" inspired them to "just say yes."

To complicate matters, for some children project D.A.R.E. was immensely effective. Just as there is ample evidence that suggests D.A.R.E. was not effective *for the general population*, there are many stories of students who, after participating in school-based D.A.R.E. activities, were sufficiently deterred from drug use and who, were it not for the D.A.R.E. officer that visited their school, might have gravitated toward recreational drug use.

And so, upon closer inspection, D.A.R.E., an initiative intended for one purpose (preventing drug use), resulted in different outcomes. Often policies or initiatives are not all good or all bad. Now, this realization alone is not a novel or even interesting assertion. What we find to be much *less* obvious and much *more* interesting, however, is the idea of policy *backfire*, which occurs when a policy or action (e.g., D.A.R.E.) designed to solve or eliminate a problem (drug use) inadvertently exacerbates it (increases drug use). It is just one potential outcome of social intervention or policy. And lucky for you, it is the subject of this book. Indeed, the purpose of this book is to investigate this dark and often unacknowledged aspect of policy implementation. In particular, the goal of this book is to shine a light on just a few of the many ways in which problematic areas in education—such as equity, disenfranchisement, and marginalization—have actually been worsened by the very policies designed to fix them.

THE NATURE OF BACKFIRE

The word *backfire* brings intense visuals to mind: a car with flames coming out of the exhaust pipe, or maybe images of Elmer Fudd covered in soot after his rifle blows up in his face (that pesky wabbit!). But what is backfire when applied to social interventions and policies like D.A.R.E.? Well, it isn't just failure, and not even phenomenal failure. Rather, backfire occurs when a policy or intervention has the *exact opposite effect* of what it was intended to do. Policies that backfire are distinct from policies that fail or even policies that have unintended consequences. Failed policies may not work, but they also don't have any *harmful* unintentional consequences or surprise outcomes. Unintended "consequences" aren't necessarily bad—they can also be good. While backfire is included under this umbrella of policies with unintended consequences, it has its own special category. In the language of children just learning to classify, all thumbs are fingers, but not all fingers are thumbs; in this instance unintended effects are the fingers, and backfire the thumbs. And they are very clumsy, awkward, unfortunate thumbs. While unintended effects can be positive or negative, backfire is always negative.

But why do we need to specifically identify policies that backfire? While unintended effects often provoke a "We should have seen that coming" face-palm moment and require a reworking of the program, and failure requires an entirely new policy or program (or not, depending on how stubborn the "deciders" may be), backfire suggests a fundamental misstep in the program design that failed to account for some vitally important factor, whatever its basis. This design flaw led to the program not just failing, not just having unintended effects, but having a genuinely iatrogenic effect, or creating greater harm as a result of the treatment. All social and educational policies are intended to do good, so the understanding of how and why they go wrong is essential to eliminating or at least decreasing the chances of this happening in the future.

With all of this said, talk is cheap. It is easy for us to write about policy backfire, to classify it, organize it, detail it, and speak of it like we have it under control. The reality is, however, that we know very little about backfire. This is because backfire, at least in the context of social policy, arises out of complexity and politics. Policies are notoriously convoluted social contracts that are (hopefully) the result of thoughtful deliberation, planning, and coordination over long periods of time that involve many different people, groups, and cultures. Think, for instance, of the complexity of the Affordable Care Act (ACA), President Obama's policy to overhaul the American health-care system. The actual law is nearly one thousand pages long. Consider how many experts and advisors were needed to craft the legislation. Then think of the number of people and organizations that will be needed to actually implement the law. Now think of the millions of people that will be affected by the law. We can keep going, but even at this point, it is quite easy to see that policies are not black and white affairs. On the contrary, social policies are messy and complex (just like society). As a consequence, it is immensely difficult to forecast what the effects of a given policy will be. We try, but in the end it is more art than science. So when backfire occurs, it always seems to come as a surprise.

WE DIDN'T SEE THAT COMING: THE UNINTENDED CONSEQUENCES OF POLICY IMPLEMENTATION

To help distinguish policy backfire from policy failure and other unintended consequences, let's look at a few examples from recent history. We consider any outcomes associated with a particular policy implementation that were previously unforeseen by the policy makers to be unintended consequences. Unintended consequences result when policies intended for one purpose actually end up producing something else, unfortunately or fortuitously. Unintended consequences differ from policy failure and policy backfire in important ways. First, as we mentioned before, unintended consequences can be both good and bad. In other words, there is a range of potentially positive or negative valence. Policy backfire, on the other hand, is bad—all bad. Also, backfire is when a well-intentioned policy leads not just directly to self-defeating, negative effects, but to self-defeating, negative effects *in exactly the area that the policy was intended to improve.* In contrast, policy failure is when a well-intentioned policy simply does not work; it just fails. We conceptualize policy failure as not having *any* effect on the targeted issue, positive or negative. Let us clarify what we mean by unintended consequences with the following examples.

China's One Child Policy

One policy that has had a plethora of unintended consequences is China's one child policy. First adopted in 1980, this policy was intended to control population growth.[6] While it has been extremely successful in terms of keeping the population down, that has not been the only effect. The biggest consequence is that China today suffers from a female deficit. More specifically, there are approximately 40 million missing women in China.[7]

The one child policy, combined with the preference for sons and the advent of sex-detecting ultrasound technology and sex-selective abortion in the 1980s, is responsible for half of these missing women.[8] Sons are traditionally higher earners, and thus promise more economic prosperity for the family than girls. Additionally, parents can depend on sons to look after them in their old age—in China daughters traditionally move into their husband's home and care for his family—so if a couple can have only one child there is a much greater preference for males.[9] These were some of the major factors behind the prioritization of sons over daughters that contributed to this female deficit.

There are some Chinese families who chose to avoid the one child policy by not registering the birth of one of their children. The grave disadvantage of this decision is that these unregistered children have no identity and no rights from the state's point of view. They are not eligible for health care, education, or lawful employment. Additionally, many women who gave birth to girls first would give these children up for adoption. There was also a high rate of female infanticide before the sex-detecting ultrasounds became readily available.[10]

Another unfortunate consequence of the one child policy is that there are few young people to take care of China's increasingly older population.[11] There are also grave psychological repercussions for men who cannot find a wife as a result of the female deficit. They are more likely to have low self-esteem and to be depressed and withdrawn. Contrary to some concerns, however, they do not show a marked increase in criminal or aggressive behavior, nor has the sex trade increased.[12]

But it's not all bleak: there are benefits to both the one child policy and the female deficit in China. Having fewer children means both children and their parents often receive better nutrition and health care, as there are "fewer mouths to feed," as the saying goes. Only children also have greater access to education than children from multiple-child households; they have completely eliminated the gender gap in educational attainment in China.[13] Additionally, as the number of women in China has gone down, their social status has gone up, which is beneficial both for their mental health and economic well-being.[14]

Although there was concern among researchers that having so many only children would lead to a country full of spoiled adults, all suffering from the "Little Emperor Syndrome," in fact these only children have been found to be more advanced in their social skills than their peers with siblings; they are more likely to have new friends, more likely to be easygoing, and less likely to be lonely. So while the unanticipated effects of the one child policy have been numerous, not all of them have been bad.

To summarize, China's one child policy (which was relaxed in 2013) did achieve its intended goal of population control, but it has also had numerous unintentional consequences. While some of those effects are negative (e.g., the female deficit, psychological suffering for some unmarried men, lack of available caregivers for elders), this is not an example of backfire. Backfire would be if the one child policy had somehow led to population growth, negating its primary purpose.

Virginity Pledges

In the last twenty years, so-called virginity pledges have proliferated around the country. Simply put, virginity pledges involve young adults "pledging" to wait until marriage to begin sexual activity. Virginity pledges are an outgrowth of abstinence-only sex education and in most cases are affiliated with Evangelical Christian traditions. One such example is Silver Ring Thing, which as a Christian ministry provides pledgers with a silver ring to be "worn as the symbol and constant reminder of a commitment before God to walk in purity and wait until marriage."[15] Pledgers give their rings to their partners after marriage as a symbol of their purity and virginity. Research into the effectiveness of virginity pledges has found little support for the idea that pledging to wait until marriage before engaging in sexual activity works.[16] Interestingly, however, making the pledge appears to be associated with unexpected and certainly unintended behavior: a number of studies into virginity pledges like Silver Ring Thing have found that young adults who pledge to wait until marriage are actually less likely than their nonpledging counterparts to use condoms and other methods of contraception when they begin engaging in sexual activity.[17] As a result, pledgers may be indeed postponing sexual activity relative to nonpledgers, but they face equal risk of sexually transmitted infections (STIs).[18] One possible explanation is that young adults who pledge but engage in premarital sexual activity are less prepared and educated about safe sexual behavior. In addition, some studies have found that pledgers may substitute other forms of sex as a way of remaining a "technical virgin."[19]

Clearly, the creators of the virginity pledge did not intend for young adults to be less likely to wear condoms during sexual activity. And they certainly did not intend for pledgers to engage in other, riskier sexual behaviors in order to be both sexually active and still chaste! In our eyes, this is a clear case of a program having unintended consequences. We would not say the program failed, because there was an effect or consequence. In fact, studies into virginity pledges have found that pledgers *are* more likely to postpone or delay sexual activity than nonpledgers (which is a success). We also would not go so far as to say the program backfired because, despite its unexpected consequences, the virginity pledges did not increase premarital sexual activity.

The Affordable Care Act

We can look to the recent passage of the Affordable Care Act, also known among its critics as "Obamacare," for another example of a policy having an unintended consequence or effect. As you may know, the ACA has been highly controversial among the American electorate. Republican members of Congress claim the ACA will cause health insurance premiums to rise and in the long term will harm the US economy by imposing heavy burdens on small-business owners and markets. Democratic lawmakers who support the ACA argue the opposite, of course. The debate in the country has been contentious at times and highly divisive. However, this debate was given new energy in 2013 when the nonpartisan Congressional Budget Office (CBO), the federal agency responsible for providing the legislative branch financial and budgetary information, projected an unintended consequence of the ACA, namely that "the number of jobs in the economy will be smaller than it would be in the absence of the ACA."[20] In fact, the CBO projected that the ACA will result in roughly 2.5 million fewer American workers choosing to participate in the labor market. Here's why. First, the ACA provides subsidies for health insurance to many low-income Americans. But once a person begins to work more and/or earn more, that individual may no longer be eligible for the subsidy. Therefore, the CBO projected that some low-income workers may choose to work less in order to continue receiving their health-care subsidy. Second, the CBO estimated that Americans who work in order to receive health insurance from their employers may decide to no longer work, to instead work part-time, or to simply retire and receive health care from their state exchange. This, the CBO projected, would result in fewer full-time-equivalent workers *choosing* to participate in the labor market.

Republican critics seized on the CBO report and held it up as proof that the ACA would wreak havoc on the already fragile US economy. Democratic proponents defended the legislation by saying that a reduced labor market wasn't harmful in the long term. The CBO stood

by its projections that the ACA would diminish labor market participation but said that it was misleading to characterize the reduction
in the labor market as "job losses" because Americans were choosing
to no longer work, which the CBO argued could be a good thing. At
any rate, the effect here (a net reduction in the labor market) was not
envisioned by the designers of the ACA. It was an unintended consequence, one that has been characterized as both positive and negative, depending on whom you speak with or which cable news shows
you choose to watch. This is not a case of policy backfire; backfire in
this context would have occurred if the number of people receiving
health insurance coverage actually decreased in the aggregate and/or
health insurance became more expensive than it was prior to the ACA
(a claim with some merit). We would not consider the ACA an example of policy failure either, because its overarching goal was to make
health care more widely available to Americans and, while some people have actually lost their personal health insurance as a result of the
ACA, the general consensus is that the ACA has increased the number
of people with health insurance coverage, especially those who previously were ineligible for coverage because of a preexisting condition.

BACK TO THE DRAWING BOARD:
WHEN POLICIES SIMPLY DO NOT WORK

Policy failure is characterized by, well, failure. For instance, if a given
policy or program was intended to have a specific outcome and after implementation and evaluation it is determined that the expected
outcome was not met, we would classify this as policy failure. It is
important to reiterate that in some cases, a policy can fail and also
have unintended consequences or even backfire, which is a special
case of unintended consequence. Yet not all cases of unintended consequences can be classified as failures. As we just learned, the ACA
has certainly had a number of unintended consequences, only one of
which we discussed, but the prevailing assessment is that the ACA,

while a highly contentious and divisive policy, is not a failed policy. It has had its intended effect, as of this writing. To explain what policy failure looks like in more detail, let's explore a few examples.

The Food Pyramid

One example of a program failing to reach its intended effect is the US Department of Agriculture's (USDA) classic, though now much maligned, food pyramid. The food pyramid was introduced by the USDA in 1992 as a way of instructing Americans about healthy eating habits. The pyramid separated foods into groups, which were divided into recommended daily serving sizes. The implication was that foods at the pyramid's base (breads and grains) were to be consumed more than those at the pyramid's peak (fats, oils, and sweets). The logic behind the pyramid was that providing Americans with a visual depiction of their daily diet would help reduce the growing rates of obesity, diabetes, and heart disease in the nation. Yet, in the years that the USDA released the food pyramid, rates of obesity actually increased. While some have speculated that the food pyramid itself was to blame for the spike in obesity (a case of backfire), the general consensus among experts is that it simply had no effect on the nation's dietary habits. In other words, it failed. But why? Well, for starters, it was confusing to both children and adults. It was at once seemingly convoluted and simplistic. The USDA updated the pyramid in 2005 as a result; however, the new "MyPyramid" rollout was derided by nutrition experts even more. If the intent of USDA and the food pyramid was to educate Americans about healthy nutrition and diet, by most quantitative measures the pyramid appears to have had zero net effect. Today, more than two-thirds of Americans are considered overweight; more than one-third are obese.[21] While the rates of obesity may have stabilized recently, America continues to have the greatest rate of obesity in the developed world. And in the years since the rollout of the food pyramid, the obesity rate among those aged fifteen and over increased from roughly 22 percent to nearly 35 percent.[22]

To be fair, the food pyramid was never expected to solve the nation's dietary and health challenges *on its own*. It would be naïve to think that simply asking Americans to eat more oatmeal would eliminate heart disease in the population. So the fact that obesity and heart disease have become so deadly is not the fault of the food pyramid. It didn't fail there. After all, the goal of the food pyramid was to educate Americans, not to improve health outcomes directly. But did the food pyramid help to educate Americans on how to eat healthily? Health experts seem to think no. As a result, we would consider the pyramid to be a failure.

Why is the food pyramid program a failure and not a case of policy backfire? Well, as we briefly mentioned earlier, some researchers and scientists have made the argument that the food pyramid *did* backfire. These researchers argue that the pyramid instructed Americans to consume way too many carbohydrates and not enough healthy oils and fats, and as a result, Americans had an unbalanced and unhealthy diet for decades. They contend that this fact, combined with the increasingly sedentary habits of the nation, actually caused the growth in the national rates of obesity and diet-related health issues. This is not the prevailing assessment, however. More evidence suggests that the food pyramid just did not work, which is why the USDA tried again with MyPyramid in 2005, and even more recently, with the "MyPlate" program in 2014. Were there any unintended consequences of the food pyramid? Perhaps. It is likely that the designers of the original food pyramid did not intend to steer Americans away from all fats and healthy oils, as some nutrition experts have argued the food pyramid did. But to us, the food pyramid best represents a case of policy failure, where a program designed for a specific set of outcomes very obviously failed to achieve those outcomes.

The War on Drugs

The war on drugs, an initiative of the Reagan administration, is perhaps the costliest example of failure we have. It is one of those instances in which public policy spawned popular concern, rather than the other way around. Prior to the war on drugs, 25 percent of the local, state, and federal prison population was incarcerated due to a drug offense; by 1996 that number had rocketed to 60 percent. In 2015, 48 percent of the federal prison population was incarcerated for drug-related offenses.[23] In 2010, the US spent over $80 billion on corrections expenditures at the federal state and local levels, not including the lost tax revenue from those incarcerated.[24]

The Anti-Drug Abuse Act of 1986 and the Anti-Drug Abuse Act of 1988 imposed harsh prison sentences for drug use, and even more merciless repercussions. The idea behind these policies was that harsh consequences would dissuade people from committing these offenses. So did they? The answer is a resounding no. These harsh penalties have been found to have little to no effect on crime. Illegal drug use was actually already decreasing prior to the start of the war on drugs, so any decrease may simply be a continuation of that trend.[25] There is no evidence that imprisonment reduced the risk of recidivism. If anything it increased it, as incarcerated inmates lost connections with their families and communities and became less employable. More recent studies on drug treatment courts found that not only are drug court participants less likely to recidivate than those incarcerated, but they are also more likely to find employment.[26]

The assumption is that when people get out of prison they will turn their lives around out of fear of being reincarcerated. Unfortunately, because zero tolerance laws deprive people who have been incarcerated for drug-related felonies of their right to government assistance in areas from public housing to education loans to food stamps, it is extremely difficult for them to find any legitimate way to work and live after their release.[27]

The war on drugs has also had harmful racial effects. While Whites represent the majority of drug offenders, they are less likely to be arrested and, if arrested, less likely to be convicted than African Americans or Hispanics, leading to a disproportionate number of minorities in prison for drug-related offenses. If current growth rates continue, by 2020 more than six in ten African American men between the ages of eighteen and thirty-four will be incarcerated.[28]

So why, despite the failure of the war on drugs and its negative effects on our society, do we continue to spend billions of dollars per year on investigations, arrests, trials, and incarcerations? Even states such as Colorado and Washington, which have begun relaxing drug laws, still have prisoners incarcerated for possession or distribution of a drug like marijuana—which is now legal in those states. At what point can we admit failure? After that much expenditure, are we even willing to do so?

The war on drugs was intended to decrease possession, distribution, and use of drugs through the fear of harsh consequences, but there has been no real decrease in any of these areas, marking these policies as true failures. Instead these policies have overburdened our prison system, leading to huge increases in the number of inmates and their likelihood of recidivism, as well as detrimental social effects in minority communities. While these are unintended effects, the complete failure of the war on drugs in its intended area—reduction of crime—warrants its classification as an abject policy failure.

ADDING FUEL TO THE FIRE: POLICY BACKFIRE

So finally we arrive at policy backfire. This special subset of unintended consequences is when a policy specifically not only fails at the area it was intended to improve or affect, but actually has the opposite result, making the problem or malady more acute. If the war on drugs had increased drug use, or if following the food pyramid made people more obese, these would be cases of backfire. While failed policies simply fail in whatever they were intended to achieve, and policies with unintended consequences have good or bad effects in addition to what they were designed to address, policies that backfire harm in exactly the area where they were intended to do good. They are the pinnacle of policies gone awry, and must be studied and understood in order to prevent their reoccurrence. Let's examine some examples of backfire.

Prohibition

One of the most infamous instances of backfire in American policy is that of Prohibition, made into the law of the land on January 16, 1919, with the ratification of the Eighteenth Amendment. Prohibition went into effect the following year after the passage of the Volstead Act, which defined "intoxicating liquor" as anything with an alcohol content greater than 0.5 percent, omitting medicinal and sacramental alcohols. It also set up the (arguably unenforceable) guidelines for both state and federal enforcement.[29] Prohibition was both an ideological and social reform inspired by the Anti-Saloon League (ASL) and churchgoers who believed that alcohol and the saloon were the root cause of much poverty and crime. The theory was that outlawing alcohol would reduce crime rates, poverty, and alcohol-related deaths.[30] Unfortunately, this "noble experiment" didn't just fail but backfired severely, increasing crime and alcohol use while poverty and alcohol-related deaths showed no improvement whatsoever.[31]

The Eighteenth Amendment did not outlaw the consumption of alcohol, only its production, distribution, and sale, so while the market demand for alcohol remained constant, the legal supply suffered. This situation created an opportunity for the mob, which had just begun to obtain a foothold in major cities. The bootlegging mobsters of the Prohibition period have since become the stuff of American legend, such as Al Capone, whose ruthless domination over Chicago's alcohol market and the ensuing territorial wars and homicides served to not only increase crime but also set the stage for an organized criminal system that persists today.[32] The American crime rate actually decreased in the late nineteenth and early twentieth centuries, but this trend was reversed by the onset of Prohibition. While minor crimes such as swearing and vagrancy ostensibly decreased during Prohibition, major crimes such as burglaries, larcenies, and assaults increased by over 20 percent.[33] The homicide rate in large cities increased from 5.6 per every 100,000 inhabitants during the first decade of the 1900s, to 8.4 during the second decade with the first wave of state alcohol restrictions, to 10 during Prohibition.[34] Following the repeal of Prohibition with the Twenty-First Amendment in 1933, the homicide rate fell from 10 to 8.3 per 100,000, suggesting a direct cause-and-effect relationship.[35] Though the reframing of alcohol as a black-market good was intended to suppress crime, it actually had the opposite effect, creating an opening for organized crime to move in, and in many cases contributing to the corruption of local politicians who were firmly in the mob's pocket.[36] Probably not what the ASL and churchgoers intended.

But what about the alcohol the bootleggers and rumrunners were providing? Prohibition marked a change in American drinking habits, moving from the less alcoholic beer to the more alcoholic spirits.[37] Additionally, drinking's new illegal status meant it took place in a freer atmosphere. That, along with the decreased social restrictions for women, led to public consumption of alcohol becoming a co-ed rather than single-sex pursuit.[38]

There were few production standards during Prohibition, with many amateurs brewing "bathtub gin" or liquor containing dangerous adulterants that could harm the drinker. In 1925 over four thousand people died from poisoned liquor, compared to slightly over one thousand in 1920.[39] People also drank more dangerously, with a gradual increase in the number of drunk driving arrests throughout Prohibition, followed by a dramatic decrease in arrest numbers after its repeal.[40] Even those who abstained from the speakeasies managed to obtain liquor, as many people turned to their doctors for their liquid courage; there was a huge increase in "legitimate" alcohol use, with doctors and hospitals doubling the amount of alcohol they sold from 1923 to 1931. The sale of medicinal alcohol (which was 95 percent pure alcohol content) increased by 400 percent during this period as well.[41]

So while the main goal of Prohibition was to decrease alcohol consumption, it backfired tremendously, with alcohol consumption increasing post-1922 to almost surpass pre-Prohibition levels prior to Prohibition's repeal in 1933.[42] What is perhaps even more remarkable is that alcohol consumption was already falling prior to the ratification of the Eighteenth Amendment; the quantity of alcohol purchased in the United States fell by approximately 20 percent between 1910 and 1920.[43] Rather than emphasizing the previously existing trend of decreased consumption, the enactment of Prohibition seemed to make drinking more enticing to Americans, reversing this trend entirely.

So while Prohibition may be labeled simply a failure in its total inability to alter the number of alcohol-related deaths or the productivity and poverty of workers, it is far more than a failure in its most critical goals of reducing both crime and alcohol consumption.[44] For these goals Prohibition backfired in the fullest meaning of the word, where the policy harms and makes worse the very thing it is intended to solve. The illegalization of "the demon rum" exacerbated the problems of crime and alcohol consumption, increasing not only crime but its severity, organization, and spread, and increasing not only alcohol consumption but the toxicity of alcohol consumed, the dangerous behavior surrounding consumption, and the social acceptability of settings in which alcohol could be consumed. In April 1933 Congress amended the Volstead Act to legalize 3.2 percent alcoholic beer, and later that year passed the Twenty-First Amendment, ending the "noble experiment" on December 3, 1933, to much greater popular enthusiasm than the Eighteenth Amendment ever encountered.[45]

Environmental Conservation

There are a number of examples of policy backfire from science, and environmental conservation in particular. For example, a recent analysis of a policy to slow the overfishing on tropical reefs off the coast of Kiribati in the central Pacific found that paying fishermen to pick coconuts instead of fishing actually caused *more* fishing. The reason was that fishermen who were persuaded to pick and sell coconuts earned more money in their new coconut ventures. That seemed like a good thing, right? Well, it was—in theory. But in practice, what happened was that these fishermen decided to work less since the coconut industry was so lucrative. And how did these newly successful former-fishermen-turned-coconut-farmers spend their free time? Why, fishing, of course! It turns out that paying fishermen to not fish actually caused them to fish more.[46] The result was an increased problem of overfishing and coral reef destruction. But backfire doesn't stop there. A similar result happened when conservation scientists decided to take action in order to preserve the fragile ecological balance on Australia's Macquarie Island.

The problem was two invasive species on this island: cats and rabbits. Feral cats were introduced to the island in the early 1800s. Rabbits came later. The cats on this island preyed on the rabbits and were so successful that they soon began running short of rabbits to eat. So the cats then turned their attention to the native birds on the island, and again were very successful. The bird species on the island were nearly exterminated. As a result, scientists decided to kill off the cats in order to protect the birds. In less than two decades all the felines on the island were shot or poisoned. No more cats. This was good news for the native bird population. But because the cats were gone, the remaining rabbits were allowed to reproduce like, well, rabbits, and the rabbit population began to resurge. The result? Environmental and ecological devastation. The out-of-control rabbits ate many plants, some of which exist only in this part of the world, bare. This led to erosion, landslides, and general ecological degradation.[47] It also made the island less habitable to the native birds. So on this World Heritage Site, ecological imbalance was hastened and made worse by a policy designed specifically to provide balance. In other words, actions taken to preserve the ecology helped to threaten it.

These two examples from conservation serve as great illustrations of policy backfire because in both cases the problems the policy designers were trying to mitigate were directly exacerbated by the policies themselves. If these were cases of policy failure, the levels of overfishing or the rates of soil erosion would have remained as they were before the policy makers decided to intervene. There would have been no change, in other words. But that is not what happened: the rates of overfishing and erosion actually increased. And because this is a bad thing considering the stated goals of the two policies, we can't label this an unintended consequence, which as you will recall can be both good and bad and in either case not necessarily related to the original malady. Let's look at another case of backfire for more clarity.

Gun Control

If we wade into the acrimonious waters of the debate over gun control in the United States, we again see signs of backfire, though in this case the backfire was not the result of any actual, tangible policy action, but merely the threat or suggestion of it. Let us explain.

Americans have always had a love of guns; the United States ranks the highest in the world in terms of firearm ownership per capita. Yet a number of recent tragedies—including the senseless and horrible 2012 shooting at Sandy Hook Elementary School, where a lone gunman killed twenty children and six adults—have led a number of politicians, including President Barack Obama, to *consider* stricter gun control laws such as universal background checks and banning the sale and use of assault-type weapons and high-capacity magazines. Yet, even though the US Congress rejected a bill that would have increased background checks following Sandy Hook, and even though a Clinton-esque assault weapons ban is similarly politically untenable for supporters of gun control today, gun sales have increased dramatically in the years following Sandy Hook. In fact, one estimate is that since 2008, when President Obama was first elected, the gun industry has grown by $9 billion in gun and ammo sales.[48] And this is without the passage of *actual laws* restricting firearms. It seems that by merely discussing his desire for increased gun control, President

Obama inadvertently inspired more gun sales. And this makes sense, in a weird way. According to one *Business Insider* article, "To be clear, gunmakers don't benefit from tighter gun control. They benefit when there are talks of tighter gun control *but those talks go* nowhere."[49] This is exactly what happened following the tragedy at Sandy Hook. In fact, gun ownership in the United States has never been higher. Since Obama has taken office, the number of states allowing for concealed carry permits has increased. There is even more vocal support in favor of open carry laws, which grant a person permission to visibly carry a firearm in any public place. Most recently, in 2014 Georgia passed the "Safe Carry Protection Act"—known among critics as the "Guns Everywhere" bill—which allows Georgians to carry firearms into bars, schools, and certain government buildings. By the end of 2013, the FBI reported that it performed over 21 million background checks for firearm purchases. Eight of the ten highest weeks for the national background system were in 2013, the year following the Sandy Hook Elementary School shooting.

The reason we consider this to be an example of backfire and not failure is that the data do not support the idea of "no effect" or a failure to meet intended outcomes (i.e., reduce gun ownership, slow the spread of firearms, increase safety). For many gun buyers, the fear of increased gun control is the driving force behind their purchase. And if it is fair to assume the Obama administration would prefer a reduction in gun sales, then the increase in gun sales is not a positive outcome and therefore cannot be a case of an unintended consequence. Let's look at one more example.

#AskSeaWorld

Not long ago, SeaWorld was a massively popular theme park. Families traveled from around the world to view orca whales and dolphins at SeaWorld's parks in San Diego, San Antonio, and Tampa. However, following the release of the 2013 documentary *Blackfish*, which documented the harsh conditions in which SeaWorld keeps some of its most popular animals, the number of visitors to the parks plummeted. In 2014 alone the stock price of SeaWorld dropped 50 percent. It is an understatement to say that, at least at the moment of this writing, SeaWorld has a very critical public relations problem. Similar public relations crises have plagued other brands: McDonalds, Jack in the Box, Marlboro, and Exxon come to mind. Some organizations have been able to rally and "weather the storm," whether through slick marketing or a forgetful consumer base or both. Some have not. The executives at SeaWorld certainly wanted to be among the former. So to combat its growing reputation as a nefarious, secretive, orca-torturing, publicly traded corporation, SeaWorld began an Internet-based marketing campaign focused around transparency and openness. The "SeaWorld Cares" campaign had a presence on virtually every hip social media platform (a clever idea to lure back the many heartbroken Millennials who saw *Blackfish* on Netflix), including Twitter, where SeaWorld established the #AskSeaWorld hashtag for people to ask questions related to marine conservation, breeding, or even *Blackfish*. The thinking, the goal, was for SeaWorld to regain control of the narrative, to calm the resentment toward the corporation, and to show that, indeed, "SeaWorld Cares." The problem was that the @SeaWorld Twitter handle quickly became the go-to place for SeaWorld bashing. In a short time SeaWorld received a torrent of attacks from other Twitter users, which begat more attacks. #AskSeaWorld soon became a breeding ground for resentment toward the brand. It essentially became an Internet version of protest against SeaWorld. And in this case, it was SeaWorld that provided users with the space to do it. Moderators of @SeaWorld even had to go as far as blocking certain Twitter users from posting to the handle. Considering the point of the campaign was to *increase* transparency, and SeaWorld had to begin censoring people, it is pretty clear #AskSeaWorld was an epic backfire.

This is a clear case of backfire because the implementation of the #AskSeaWorld hashtag resulted in increased hostility toward

SeaWorld. SeaWorld unknowingly gave its harshest critics a space to congregate and to drown out any positive messages the company was hoping would be the focus. SeaWorld's image took another hit once people learned the moderators of @SeaWorld were censoring some of the most vocal (and rude) critics; the company now seemed like a bully. Failure in this case would have a null effect. The #AskSeaWorld strategy would have failed if the hashtag didn't improve or worsen the brand's image. But that was not the case. It was also not the case that a positive result came about from the #AskSeaWorld idea. Yes, perhaps there was a drop of positive imaging among the bucketful of negativity SeaWorld received, but that is all. The program backfired in a very hurtful way for the brand.

POLICY BACKFIRE IN EDUCATION

At its core, the schooling system in the United States is touted as the key way in which disenfranchised, underrepresented, and "at-risk" populations can move up the ladder—socially and economically. Therefore it comes as no surprise that much of the educational policy-making time and resources is devoted to supporting student populations who are falling behind in school. These populations often include (but are not limited to) students of color, low-income families, low academic performers, students with disabilities, and those in failing schools. Over the past decades, we have seen an influx of state and educational policies designed in a way to reduce educational gaps and promote access and success for these groups by improving schooling structures and practices. While these policies have been diverse in approach, they are often united in asking how we can better improve schools to serve the needs of diverse student populations.

Yet many of these schooling policies have backfired; that is, policies that were explicitly intended to reduce educational gaps for disenfranchised groups through changes in schooling structures and practices have caused the reverse effect—a widening of the gaps that they had set out to close.

As we've discussed, policy and program failure, unintentional consequences, and even backfire can happen in all forms and areas, from national to local, from prisons to foods to population control. But what happens when these policies go wrong for our most vulnerable student populations? No one creates policies for schools hoping they will backfire. No lawmaker ever wakes up and decides to make things harder for some kids today—we hope. So what do we do when these policies created to help at-risk youth backfire and make things harder? How do they backfire and how do we identify and learn from these situations?

To answer these questions, this edited book presents a collection of case studies on school backfire. This is a first, unique opportunity to present a multifaceted, multidisciplinary examination of when educational policy and practice do not converge—and what lessons we can learn.

The contributing authors represent a multitude of disciplines and methodological approaches, are located across the United States, and have each studied a different geographic region and different disenfranchised group in the schooling population. Each uses a quantitative, qualitative, or synthesis approach to examine one particular case of policy backfire. In collecting these studies, this book provides a first critical and national look at the consequences of unintended policy backfire—getting at the heart of the issue of backfire through different policy-analytic approaches.

In sum, studying these cases of backfire is not only important, it is essential. Each case is unique and yet they all had the same result: total and utter failure in exactly the area these policies were designed to help. Not just failure, but catastrophic failure—a deleterious effect, creating a worse situation than the one before. Only through studying these cases, through understanding how and why backfire happened, can we hope to avoid it in the future. If we do not examine these cases and learn from them, we will keep making the same mistakes over and over, and continue to harm those whom we wish to help.

In the coming chapters eleven authors will identify six cases where backfire happened, and policies put in place to improve at-risk students' performance in a specific area had the exact opposite effect, making the situation so much worse.

ONE

When Targeted Interventions Backfire

How a Middle School Literacy Intervention Created Achievement Gaps

Shaun M. Dougherty

When is a support not a support? When it undermines the outcome it intended to improve! The increased use of standardized test scores and a focus on federal, state, and local accountability policies to drive student performance has led to the proliferation of interventions intended to improve student outcomes. In many cases such interventions have been designed to increase student exposure to core, tested subject material like mathematics and language arts instruction with the goal of improving performance, especially among students who had been lower performing.[1] Some of these educational responses have been shown to provide educational benefits; others demonstrate how the incentives espoused by formal policies may create perverse responses and thereby hurt student outcomes; and even well-intentioned programs may have unanticipated consequences.[2] In this chapter I examine the design, implementation, and impact of a middle school reading intervention that produced differential impacts on short-term measures of student performance by race. Though the program used research-based strategies to deliver a supplementary reading curriculum, the result was that White, Asian, and Latino students who were induced to participate in the program had marginally higher test score outcomes, while Black students in this district who participated in the course fared worse on these same outcomes. In this case, the policy both backfired (caused the opposite effect of its goal) and produced the unintended consequence of enrolling more students in the supplemental course than was intended. Both of these findings underscore the importance of studying policy implementation to fully understand differences in school context when deploying districtwide policies across multiple settings, and highlight the potential for policies meant to enhance learning among otherwise successful students to instead do harm.

There is no conflict in the academic literature, nor among practitioners and policy makers, regarding the salience of literacy in academic preparation. Very few elements of educational research and practice enjoy such agreement, and such an unambiguous body of evidence suggesting that early literacy development is paramount among the factors associated with future academic and social success.[3] Some of this agreement arises from studies that link literacy rates and incarceration rates or employment data, while other evidence comes from rigorous research that demonstrates how high-quality instruction and particular pedagogical approaches can improve literacy skills when compared to baseline or "business as usual" approaches.[4] Out of this agreement has emerged a wealth of knowledge about how to teach students to improve multiple measures of literacy attainment and skill, and how those approaches should differ by demonstrated need and development. For instance, there is a strong and established understanding of how to instruct adolescents in a way that is optimal for them, which differs from how we might instruct an elementary-age student.[5]

In addition to a well-developed literature on the potential to impact literacy development, there is a growing literature on how offering additional learning time (particularly in tested areas) impacts student outcomes. Several papers have demonstrated how longer school years or more days of instruction based on fewer unanticipated interruptions (e.g., snow days) lead to better student learning outcomes.[6]

As an outgrowth of this work, there has been a proliferation of school policies that expand student instructional time in certain subjects.[7] These types of programs fall primarily into two types: those focused on remediating perceived areas of need, and those that seek to promote academic advancement.[8] Many of these policies respond to the incentives created under No Child Left Behind (NCLB), Race to the Top, and waivers to NCLB. Others, however, have taken an approach that focuses on longer-run measures of success, such as college preparation and growing the college-going pipeline for students who are initially near average performance on nationally normed measures.[9] The policy detailed here, and the focus of this chapter, is one such example. The results of this policy highlight potential caveats of such a strategy, and underscore the importance of taking a nuanced approach to designing and deploying policies, particularly those developed at the district level and that apply across multiple school contexts. It is precisely the variation in the school contexts within this district that likely contributes to the potentially harmful effects of this policy on Black students.

CONTEXT AND POLICY

As in many school districts nationwide, Hampton County Public Schools (HCPS; a pseudonym) recognizes the importance of literacy skills in ensuring the academic and long-term success of its students. Decades of research supports such a focus.[10] And a substantial body of knowledge has been amassed to document what strategies and practices are effective in promoting the literacy skills of learners of many ages and backgrounds.[11] Long before the Common Core State Standards focus on college and career readiness, the literacy education policies of HCPS included a focus on ensuring that the district's high school graduates are prepared to succeed in college. That commitment includes identifying students who are on the margin of being well prepared for college as early as middle school and finding ways to support their success. The policy this chapter examines is a previous iteration of the current program that focuses on using an objective criterion to identify students whose reading skills are not yet consistent with those of students who in earlier cohorts were able to gain entrance into and succeed in college.

After identifying the students who were not meeting the college-ready guidelines, the district offered these students a spot in a literacy support class beginning in sixth grade, the start of middle school. The literacy support class was designed to be taken in place of an exploratory world language course that most students would take in middle school. Since more competitive colleges require multiple years of a world language in high school as part of the admissions criteria, there could be some concern that the district policy would limit student access to world language course taking; however, even students who took three full years of the literacy support class in middle school could take four years of a world language once they enrolled in high school. In this way the supplemental literacy course worked as a substitute for a world language, but only in the short term.

One of the largest districts in the nation, HCPS is a suburban district immediately adjacent to a large city, and is racially and socioeconomically diverse with nearly 40 percent each Black and White students and over 30 percent of students eligible for free- or reduced-price lunch. Despite this diversity, important patterns of residential segregation are obscured by these aggregate figures. In fact, among the nineteen middle schools in the sample for this study, several enrolled student bodies that were predominantly White or predominantly Black (where "predominantly" is defined as one group comprising more than half of the student population). These details of the racial and socioeconomic variation and the residential segregation play a salient role in the evaluation of the policy considered in this chapter.

The policy considered here used student performance on the fifthgrade Iowa Test of Basic Skills (ITBS) in reading to identify whether students would benefit from a middle school literacy course in place of what would otherwise be an elective in a world language of their choice. Students below the cutoff of the 60th national percentile on the ITBS in reading were eligible for this supplementary course, while those who scored at the 60th percentile or above were ineligible. Eligibility was meant to be unbiased since it was linked to an objective criterion. However, take-up of the course was far less simple, and contributed to the unintended consequences of the policy that are discussed later. An important element of this policy approach is that it is blind to student characteristics other than nationally normed literacy performance. Though Black students were found to have had lower levels of college participation than their White, Asian, and Latino counterparts, HCPS was aware of the importance of avoiding strategies that could unfairly target students based on race or class. Using an objective criterion to determine eligibility, the district could appear fair and not be seen as targeting students based on race or class. Conversely, by using the cutoff that it did, the policy implicitly had the potential to boost the college readiness (if successful) of more Black students than any single other group of students.

Supplemental literacy instruction for students as a means to promote college going was also part of a larger district focus on literacy. In parallel with the supplemental literacy course examined in this chapter, another policy focused on remediating the literacy skills of students who fell in the lowest performance category on the state reading assessment. In this program the cutoff score that delineated the lowest and second performance categories (both below the third category of proficient) was used to assign students to remedial coursework. However, several features of this program did not allow for it to be evaluated with a similar high-quality approach. It is worth noting, though, that the policy investigated here occurred in a dynamic and systematic policy environment focused on adolescent literacy.

It is also important to note that, in an effort to be family friendly, HCPS constructed its policy to offer supplementary literacy course-work in a manner that allowed students to either opt in if they scored just above the formal eligibility threshold, or opt out if they fell just below. Any experienced school or district administrator will tell you that this is good practice, and may be just the element needed to get schools and families to agree to such a policy. Political realities aside, the structure of this program caused at least two complications. First, from an evaluation standpoint it decreased the difference in the exposure to supplemental literacy as a function of the eligibility rule. Second, the structure of the policy allowed for differences in participation based on differences in knowledge or understanding of eligibility and participation requirements, or perceived agency to respond to that information. For instance, if White and Black families received different messages about whether and how to opt in or out of the program, then we could see differences across school contexts in participation.

DATA, SAMPLE, AND ANALYTIC APPROACH

Though HCPS had a supplemental literacy course in middle school for some time, the study on which this chapter is based relied on administrative data from the district itself for the academic years spanning the fall of 2002 through the spring of 2007. In this timeframe there were five cohorts of students who were observed beginning in fifth grade (when they took the ITBS that dictated their eligibility for the supplemental literacy course) through the eighth grade (the end of their middle school experience in this district). Data limitations prevent tracking these students any further, but this longitudinal panel allows us to observe student exposure to the literacy support class across all middle grades, to determine whether and how that exposure impacted their subsequent performance, and to understand whether these impacts affected all students similarly, or were heterogeneous by race or income status.

In this chapter, differences by race or ethnicity are highlighted. This distinction is made largely because the initial evaluation of these differences proved salient, and also because the policy context (residential patterns and school composition) suggested that such distinctions may be present and were certainly relevant to the policy. Specifically, because White and Black students made up the clear majority of students in the district (over 80 percent between both groups), with Black students experiencing some substantial residential segregation, the analysis looked at Black students as one group of interest, and White, Latino, and Asian students as a second group. While the latter group of students is not a traditional or policy-defensible combination, the decision was made for statistical purposes. Though we likely would want to know the impact of the policy on students from individual racial, ethnic, socioeconomic, or linguistic backgrounds, the dataset is not large enough to support such analysis in a responsible and valid manner. The informed hypothesis that the policy might differentially affect Black students based on patterns of residential sorting is then preferred, and all students who do not identify as Black are grouped to ensure suitable statistical power and more appropriate and defensible inferences.

The use of a cutoff or threshold value on the ITBS to determine eligibility for the supplemental literacy course, and the fact that there was real variation in whether students participated in the course as a result of this cutoff or decision rule, is what allowed for the estimation of this policy's impact on student outcomes. The evaluation relied on a fuzzy regression-discontinuity (RD) design where I first estimated a student's exposure to the supplemental literacy course as a result of the student's ITBS score and whether it fell below the 60th percentile rank of performance. I was then able to use prediction of exposure to the course to estimate the effect of taking the course on the student's subsequent test scores. For a more detailed articulation of the methods used in this evaluation, see the literature on RD designs more generally.[12]

The impact of being just eligible (relative to just missing being eligible based on the fifth-grade ITBS) on a student's take-up of the supplemental literacy course is demonstrated in figure 1.1, which presents on the vertical axis the share of total semesters in middle school (by the end of eighth grade) where a student was enrolled in the supplemental literacy course as a function of his or her ITBS reading score (horizontal axis) and its position relative to the 60th percentile cutoff used to determine eligibility (indicated by the vertical dashed line). In figure 1.1, two interrelated phenomena are immediately clear. First, the discontinuity in exposure to supplemental literacy at the cutoff is modest, demonstrated by the fact that the trend to the left of the vertical line is slightly higher than the trend just to the right. This indicates that eligibility for supplemental literacy did result in higher exposure compared to students who just missed being eligible based on the rule. The second phenomenon is that take-up of

FIGURE 1.1   Share of total semesters students spent enrolled in supplemental literacy by the end of eighth grade by fifth-grade ITBS reader score

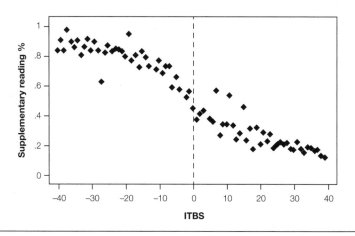

the supplemental literacy course was high among those who were not technically eligible under the policy assignment rule. That is to say that the share of total time in supplementary literacy for students who were at or above the vertical line denoting the 60th percentile in grade five was about 40 percent. Despite the fact that the difference in exposure to supplementary literacy is not huge (no big jump at the cutoff), it is statistically significant, which was enough to then use this difference in exposure to estimate the effect of exposure on later outcomes.

RESULTS

The result of the policy was twofold. First, though the policy was designed to be binding, in an effort to be more family friendly the district allowed for students to elect in and out of the requirement. As a result, the take-up of the intervention in middle school was quite fuzzy (shown in figure 1.1), which was one unintended consequence. Second, the policy produced counterintuitive results on student outcomes. Participation in this supplemental literacy course generated small positive impacts for White, Asian, and Latino students, but fairly large negative impacts for Black students. Both of these results are unpacked next, with an emphasis on describing how the results were unintended and led to a backfiring of the policy impact for Black students.

Even though district and school officials wanted the policy to be flexible and family friendly, they did not anticipate the high rates of students and their families that chose to opt either in or out depending on their eligibility status. School officials have many anecdotes to explain this behavior, some of which is documented elsewhere in the academic literature. Some people were concerned that the use of an otherwise arbitrary cutoff actually created a meaningful distinction or just induced otherwise nonexistent variation.[13] One could imagine a parent whose child was in the 59th percentile objecting to having their child assigned to the class and overriding the policy. Conversely, one can also imagine a parent whose child was at the 61st percentile preferring that the child receive the supplemental literacy course as a form of insurance. Importantly, one might also imagine how these parental responses could be systematically different among students or families that feel more or less empowered, or where parents had concerns about the quality of the additional course.[14] If families of Black or non-Black children differentially felt that being eligible or not either stigmatized or disadvantaged their child, there could be differences in compliance with the policy and take-up of the supplemental course.

In fact, though I cannot observe the reasons for the differences in take-up, there are clear differences between how Black and non-Black students took up the policy as a result of being eligible. Even more salient is that differences in take-up of supplemental literacy are even greater depending on whether a Black student was enrolled in a predominantly White or predominantly Black school. These differences in compliance likely caused considerable headaches for district- and school-level leaders who were tasked with deploying the policy. As a result, one might imagine that in addition to the flexibility about who was able to enroll (or not) in the supplemental course, there might also be differences in how the course operated for those who did participate. From a technical standpoint I was able to account for such possible differences by school and year of implementation by including school-by-year fixed effects that ensure that all comparisons are made just among students in the same school and academic year and identify effects that are the net of such site-level differences. The fact remains, though, that the design and deployment of the policy caused substantial unintended upheaval and is a salient takeaway for policy makers at the local and state levels. While the imperfect policy compliance will not come as a surprise to anyone who has spent any time in a public school, the degree to which noncompliance occurred, and the fact that it was systematically different by race in this racially bifurcated school environment, is notable.

Despite these differences in take-up and imperfect compliance with the policy as designed, I was able to identify the effects of this policy, which were also contrary to its spirit and intention. While the program was intended and designed (at least at the district level) to promote improvement in subsequent performance, the evidence pointed more strongly to a negative effect for Black students, who were already underrepresented in the district's college-going population—the expansion of which was the policy's intended goal. Interestingly, in aggregate the program appeared to have no effect on student test scores—neither those required for state accountability nor the eighth-grade measure of the ITBS in literacy. These null aggregate effects masked, however, the negative effects experienced by Black students in the district. Even more alarming is that the negative effects for Black students were clearest and more pronounced in schools where Black students constitute less than half of the school population; that is, in predominantly White schools, Black students were affected more negatively than in other settings.

The differences in the effects of the policy can be demonstrated in several ways, but one benefit of the RD design is that it lends itself to demonstrating effects graphically. Figure 1.2 presents the reduced-form effects of the supplemental literacy course by race and by school racial composition. Each of the four panels displays a graph of a student's eighth-grade reading score on the vertical axis against a student's national percentile rank in the fifth grade recentered on the cutoff of the 60th percentile (set to zero). The vertical dashed line depicts the cutoff percentile rank such that students to the left were eligible for supplementary literacy, and those to the right were not. The difference in the levels of the test score on either side of the vertical dashed line indicates the difference in the outcomes for students who were nearly identical in their fifth-grade ITBS percentile, but differed by where they fell with respect to the cutoff used in this district's policy. What is most clear is that for Black students average scores were lower among those eligible for the supplemental course,

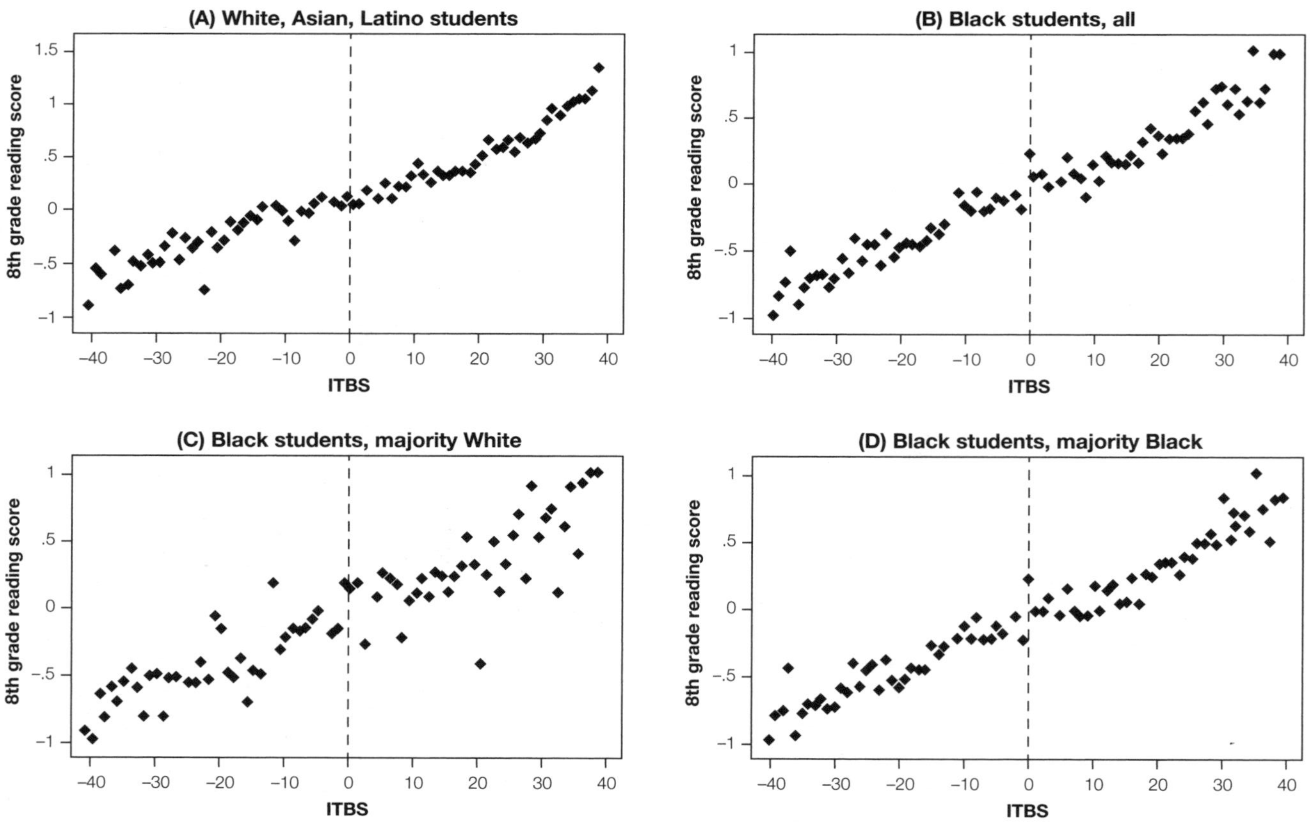

FIGURE 1.2 Effect of eligibility on eighth-grade state reading test scores by race and educational setting

relative to those just to the right of the cutoff and not eligible. This is clearest in panels (B) and (C) where the performance trajectories among those not eligible for the course (to the right of the dashed line) are higher than for those on the left, indicating that those who were not in supplementary literacy performed better at least for Black students in White majority schools. The visual evidence is less clear for White, Asian, and Latino students, but is suggestive of slightly higher performance trends on the lefthand side among those in supplemental literacy.

A full consideration of how to estimate and interpret these differences is given in Dougherty (2015), but for our purposes here the key takeaways are that: (1) aggregate analyses suggest there is no effect, and (2) the actual effects run counter to what was intended, especially for Black students who constitute a large share of students, and who were a focal group of interest in this policy setting.

BACKFIRE AND UNINTENDED CONSEQUENCES

The policy backfired in two ways. First, though the policy was designed so that the eligibility rule would be followed, the district allowed students to elect in or out of the requirement. Because the policy in practice was not compulsory, participation in the intervention was not in strict accordance with the assignment rule (from this, program evaluation implications will be discussed). Second, the intervention tended to produce small positive impacts for White, Asian, and Latino students who just qualified for the program, but medium to large negative impacts for Black students. Therefore, the reading intervention program that set out to improve performance had the reverse effect—negatively impacting the performance of some students—and created a gap between Black and White eligible students where previously there was not one! Further concerning is that for Black students in predominantly White schools, the policy tended to be more binding for Black students, and the negative effects were most pronounced, exacerbating concerns about the role of race in the policy's impact.

Technical Backfire

The main reason for the first element of the backfire appears to have been a myopic focus on using an objective criterion that could be applied districtwide, without thinking about how this cutoff would behave differently in different schools. This research emphasizes that while districtwide policies that rely on test score cutoffs may appear to be unbiased, they may operate differentially at the school level and have important and unintended consequences for the students in those schools. Such impacts may be more pronounced in schools and districts where there are starkly contrasting racial and socioeconomic characteristics. Specifically, the use of a national percentile criterion for eligibility meant that within-school distributions of ITBS percentiles differed substantially by school. As noted earlier, I found that for Black students in predominantly White schools, where the policy tended to be more binding for those students, the negative effects were most pronounced.

How did the criterion operate differently across school settings? If we simulate test score distributions by race, and incorporate the knowledge that the mean performance for Black students is lower, on average, than for White students, we could generate a distribution such that the same cutoff (60th percentile nationally) would cut the Black distribution by race much differently. In particular, the cutoff would slice through a denser portion of the Black distribution than the White distribution, leading to two unanticipated (but anticipatable) outcomes that would follow from mechanistically implementing the policy: more Black students than White students would be identified for the supplementary course, and there would be less racial balance in the supplemental course versus a typical course for students of the same ability in the school at large. These outcomes would not be as noticeable at a predominantly Black school because the population and distribution of scores for White, Asian, and Latino students would be much lower, but in predominantly White schools it could be quite pronounced. In fact, this very reality played out in Hampton County.

Could this technical form of backfire have been avoided? In principle, having a universal cutoff on an objective criterion operate differently for two different groups of students across multiple school settings could be anticipated. However, it is easy to make this claim thirteen years after the fact. In fact, 2002 was in the early stages of high-stakes testing, when schools were trying to build responsive and fair policies to support student learning. Though test scores were used in this district for many purposes, the development of responsive policies at the district level that were applied across nineteen schools was in its infancy, and such oversights led to hard lessons learned.

Mechanisms

A reason for the second type of backfire, negative outcomes for Black participants, may be that policy makers failed to consider the effect on students of being told that they have to take a different course than their friends just because their score was below a certain cutoff. For the same reason that students who win admissions lotteries to their schools of choice may demonstrate improved attendance even before they enter that school, youth who are performing at average levels may feel disempowered if they receive a message that their performance is not as strong as that of their peers, particularly when gender, race, socioeconomic status, disability, or first language is also a factor.[15] Thus, the backfire in Hampton County might have occurred due to the inadvertent labeling of students who were above and below the policy cutoff without regard for where this cutoff fell in the distributions for important student groups. As a result, this labeling may have directly contributed to harming student performance. Thus, though the treatment was supposed to be a support class, it instead became the receipt of a negative message that students carried within them into that course.

How students perceive being categorized, even when the criteria being used to categorize them is objective, can be potentially problematic. In this case, if students experience their eligibility for the supplementary course as punitive, they may internalize that message and demonstrate lower subsequent performance not just because of the class but because of how they made sense of what put them there. Students may experience a reduction in self-efficacy and academic engagement when they receive a message that they perceive indicates poor performance (relative to their peers), which could explain why students who participated in the supplemental literacy course did worse subsequently.[16] However, the lower performance was experienced only by Black students, suggesting that another factor might be at play. This potential "negative shock" associated with being identified as a lower performer was also found by Papay and colleagues when they demonstrated that students who just fell into the lowest performance category on the state-mandated test for accountability in Massachusetts had poorer high school and college outcomes than similar students who scored just above this performance threshold.[17] Importantly, the negative effect in Massachusetts was clearest for lower-income students in cities. Thus, as in the current analysis (which used a similar strategy to identify the policy effect and illustrated comparable negative effects), the negative impacts were concentrated in a subgroup of students that policy makers and practitioners know to be more vulnerable in general.

Many scholars have studied the potential of negative messages to adversely affect the outcomes of those who receive them. Both economics and psychology offer theoretical models with empirical evidence suggesting that identity, self-perception, and efficacy likely impact how messages are received and how receipt of those messages translates into outcomes. For instance, the literature on stereotype threat suggests that groups that historically have been labeled as lower achieving tend to perform worse in conditions when they are primed to recall this history of being so labeled.[18] In economics there is also some evidence that self-perception and relative ability may impact outcomes or decisions about how students make educational investments.[19]

Another way to make sense of these negative effects is to suggest that they were not real and that students simply didn't try as hard on the test. However, the negative effects that I found in Hampton County were evident not only on state tests of accountability but also on the eighth-grade ITBS. One could imagine that if Black students experienced the supplemental course as a sign that the school system was disenfranchising them, they could have opted to exert less effort on subsequent exams since there weren't any real stakes applied to performance on those assessments for the students themselves. Of course, all students could be aware of the fact that these tests have few student-level stakes attached to them, but if Black students in predominantly White schools felt particularly disengaged by the policy, test scores could have declined in response but may not actually illustrate real differences in knowledge or ability.

Peer Effects

Students in the supplemental literacy course might also have experienced differences in the peer composition of their literacy or other courses, and these differences in peer exposure could also impact subsequent performance. Under this policy, if being in the supplemental literacy course led to a concentration of lower-ability peers (relative to students not in the course), then we might expect learning in those classrooms to be less strong than in more heterogeneous groupings, or homogenous groupings of students who previously scored higher. Recent work by Nomi (2015) found that a "double dose" of middle school literacy instruction led to slightly higher subsequent performance for students of average ability, but that the effect was mediated by peer composition.[20] She also demonstrated that the lower-ability students experienced a classroom whose peer composition was lower performing, on average, than students of higher ability. Such work underscores the potential negative effects of changes in peer composition in cutoff-based intervention policies. In this case, group data on peer composition were not available, but this is clearly an area for more good work to be done.

Use of the score cutoff to assign students to supplemental literacy could also have generated unanticipated effects on peer composition. For instance, since so many students above the cutoff opted in to the course, they accounted for some of the peers in the supplemental literacy classrooms. If noncompliers were in any way systematically noncompliant (e.g., students opting in were more likely to be of one race or another), the peer influence could look quite different than if the courses were filled only with compliers. Though any inferences attempted in HCPS would be speculative at best, recent work from Bowen (2015) illustrates how noncompliance with cutoffs under similar policies can lead to unintended differences in peer composition.[21] He found that, in Texas, students who were not eligible by virtue of scoring above the eligibility cutoff for a remedial reading program were more likely to be enrolled in the remedial program if they were also free-lunch-eligible than higher-income students with the same eligibility score. Under such a system the intervention effects on compliers could be driven by their perceptions and experiences of noncompliers who were sorted into the intervention and therefore make up part of the treatment.

Of course, even when compliance is good and there aren't grossly unanticipated outcomes, the effect of cutoff-based policies with interventions designed to enhance performance may not always result in positive effects. Math interventions that utilize a similar mechanism for identifying students who are, and are not, eligible have found positive impacts on both short- and longer-term outcomes, though there is some evidence that benefits identified by test scores may fade out quickly.[22] Conversely, the literature on the effects of literacy interventions that use cutoff scores to identify eligible students has been more mixed. Early evidence from Bowen (2015) suggests null effects, whereas in the Hampton County evaluation I found differential effects by race (Dougherty 2015).[23]

AVOIDING BACKFIRE IN TARGETED INTERVENTIONS

Despite the missteps and unintended consequences of intervention policies that backfire such as the one outlined here, there's no need to throw out the baby with the bathwater. As highlighted by Schlotter, Schwerdt, and Woessmann (2011), there is much to be learned from policies whose design supports strong quasi-experimental evaluation.[24] However, the lesson to be taken from rule-based policies like the one in Hampton County is that they are a good start for promoting objectivity in assignment, but they are not sufficient to ensure fair assignment to educational practices and programs, or—as I explore momentarily—to result in the intended outcome. In addition, it is possible that poor deployment by way of imperfect information or guidance for the eligible students could exacerbate the negative impacts. Perhaps students were not told how or why Hampton County's course assignment decision was made and why they might benefit. Alternatively, instruction in the supplemental course could have been of lower quality or not sufficiently different from the instruction in other courses to generate enthusiasm. Many of these potential concerns are addressable by policy makers and practitioners.

So what should policy makers and practitioners take from the experience of Hampton County and its rule-based literacy policy? Several factors emerge as worthy of consideration. First, know your audience. District and school leaders should be mindful of how policies will be received by their students and their families, particularly rule-based policies where people may quibble over whether smaller differences on a single score should dictate different educational experiences. Second, the devil is in the details when it comes to implementation. Failure to consider who will be impacted, and whether that impact may be differential by salient and observable characteristics (such as race, class, or gender), is a design flaw and may be avoided if all available data are leveraged in the planning process. Third, document implementation. School and district leaders have to document who is teaching, what resources are used, and what implementation looks like in the classroom if they are to make sense of what students experience relative to what was intended or planned. Fourth, evaluate, evaluate, and reevaluate. You can only assess a policy's impact on students if you have evaluated at regular intervals. While retrospective policy evaluations are better than nothing, real policy-relevant information comes from evaluating in parallel with deployment. As wise evaluators have noted, "you can't fix by analysis what you've bungled by design."[25] While the specific context of this quote is not entirely analogous to the policy currently being considered, it remains true that we cannot fully understand how something affects outcomes if we haven't planned in advance for how we will evaluate those effects.

Going forward, policy makers should carefully consider how blanket policies—even when they rely on objective criteria—can have differing impacts when they are deployed at the building level, especially where there is considerable heterogeneity in the student population across buildings. Policy makers should also keep in mind that messaging and marketing are important elements of deploying policies, and that those responsible for enacting policies that impact students must buy into the plan if the policy is to be marketed authentically and convincingly. The impacts of messaging and marketing will likely interact with individual feelings of empowerment and perceived power in these settings, so careful attention must be paid to potential power dynamics and the potential for unintended coercion.

In future work, practitioners, policy makers, and academics should partner to design prospective studies that can shed light both on the effects of cutoff-score-based policies on student outcomes and on the mechanisms that explain the presence or absence of those effects. Without such prospective planning, the educational community is likely in for a series of evaluation studies that may show conflicting evidence, the causes and mechanisms of which are largely unknown. Perhaps worst of all for practitioners, without careful consideration of how the community stakeholders will interpret the intent of the policy, they may spend more time fielding concerns about whether students will opt in or out than ensuring the deployment of a high-quality program that meets the originally intended goals.

TWO

When Accountability Policies Backfire

Why Summer Learning Loss Affects Student Test Scores

Andrew McEachin and Allison Atteberry

INTRODUCTION

One of the most prominent debates in education policy today is how to design federal, state, and local policies that hold schools accountable for student outcomes, especially in light of the decade's worth of complaints about the No Child Left Behind Act of 2001 (NCLB), a reauthorization of the 1965 Elementary and Secondary Education Act (ESEA). Performance-based accountability policies hinge on the ability to make valid and reliable inferences about schools' impact on student learning. Researchers and policy makers have grappled with how to best distinguish between schools' influence on student achievement and the myriad of external factors (i.e., those outside the schools' purview) that impact student learning. As discussed in this book's introduction, the simplistic measures of school quality and performance used in NCLB, despite some positive effects on student achievement, can largely be described as a policy backfire. To assuage these well-documented concerns over NCLB, the US Department of Education implemented a waiver program in 2011 to provide states the flexibility to design and implement new accountability systems.[1] One of the main components of this waiver program is a move to hold schools accountable not only for student achievement *levels*, but also for student achievement *growth*, through the use of growth models. These growth models generate school-level performance measures that capture schools' impact on students' achievement growth, often conditioning on student and school characteristics that are beyond the control of educators and administrators.[2]

The validity of growth models as a measure of school performance rests on a number of assumptions, many of which have been probed in existing work.[3] If these assumptions break down, then states and districts will identify the wrong schools as "failing." Mislabeling schools as failing can lead to a number of backfires, affecting the schools' ability to hire high-quality teachers, redirecting curriculum and resources to tested grades and subjects, and exaggerating stereotype bias.

Proponents hope that the use of student achievement growth models will better capture the portion of student achievement attributable to schools' policies and practices, as well as reduce the link between schools' accountability standings and external factors (e.g., student poverty), eliminating many of the concerns associated with older measures based on achievement levels.[4] However, one important but often ignored assumption posits that student scores on annual tests, usually administered each spring, measure the amount of learning attributable to a school. This metric fails to account for the fact that summer vacation constitutes approximately a quarter of the days in the typical spring-to-spring testing window, and thus has the potential to conflate the impact of schools on students' learning with learning that occurs during the summer.

Since the 1970s we have known that the summer break is a turbulent time for student learning, especially for students from traditionally underserved groups.[5] Research on summers suggests that student learning is not uniform over the summer; White and middle-class children often exhibit learning gains over this time period, while minority and/or disadvantaged children experience losses.[6] The negative impact of summer break on lower socioeconomic students is often referred to as "summer setback" or "summer learning loss." It is quite shocking, however, that the summer learning loss literature has not had an impact on the design of school accountability policies.

In sum, school accountability policies were designed to raise the performance of underachieving schools, schools that serve large shares of the nation's most vulnerable students. To address the shortcomings of the NCLB-style accountability model, federal and state policy makers have introduced the use of growth models. In this chapter, we explore how the movement to growth models still fails to capture the true impact of school on student achievement, in large part due to students' differential summer learning loss. The goal of this chapter is to combine the research on school accountability and summer setback by demonstrating how the failure to account for students' summer learning in the design and implementation of school accountability systems poses a problem for schools serving larger shares of minority and low-income students. We find that students' summer learning will in fact cause the new waiver accountability policies to backfire, by introducing bias into the growth models they typically use. This bias negatively affects the relative standing of schools serving more disadvantaged students. We close the chapter with a discussion on the implications of this policy backfire on future iterations of federal and state accountability systems.

SCHOOL ACCOUNTABILITY POLICIES

Policies that hold teachers and schools accountable for their students' outcomes have been implemented for two main reasons. The first is to solve what is known as the *principal-agent problem*. In complex settings like schools, it is impossible to monitor the daily activities of teachers and school administrators (agents). However, it is still important to ensure that their activities are aligned with the goals and interests of the broader society (principals). Proponents believe that the use of annual performance targets in school accountability policies will better align educators' behaviors with local, state, or federal standards without the need to monitor their activity on a daily basis.[7] The second reason for school accountability policies is to address market failures due to information asymmetry by infusing the educational marketplace with data about the effect of teachers and schools on student achievement and other outcomes.[8] In short, parents and the broader society do not have good data on the quality of the school system at large; they may have experience at their own or a small subset of local schools, but they lack information about overall student experiences and outcomes. Annual reports of school quality ensure that parents and other stakeholders are informed about the local and broader educational landscape, allow them to make informed decisions about where to send their children, and help policy makers allocate resources to schools in need. In both cases—the principal-agent problem and information dissemination—"performance" is generally defined, at least in part, by students' performance on achievement assessments, which presumes that test scores, despite not capturing every skill deemed important by society, are strongly related to students' future success.[9]

The ability for school accountability policies to elicit optimal behavior from educators relies on valid measures of teacher and school performance that accurately reflect educators' efforts. If these measures are too noisy, too rigid, or biased by factors outside the actors' control, the incentives to align behaviors with expectation break down and unintended consequences may emerge. For example, it is well documented that the proficiency-based measures used under NCLB, and still prevalent with the ESEA waivers, were prone to a number of validity and reliability issues.[10] The poorly designed performance measures led to maladaptive responses by teachers and administrators, including focusing on students on the margin of proficiency, narrowing the curriculum, placing low performing students in non-tested subgroups, and so on.[11]

It is debated whether these behavioral responses from families, school leaders, and teachers are beneficial to schools. However, regardless of one's take on these policy mechanisms, it is clear that *none* of these behavioral responses can be beneficial if the accountability system identifies the wrong schools as highly effective or ineffective. For instance, if the bias in school performance measures from out-of-school influences on students' achievement misidentifies schools serving larger shares of traditionally underserved students, effective teachers may avoid working with the most disadvantaged students or challenging schools.[12] Indeed, and as we have touched upon, the use of growth models in a spring-to-spring testing window may do exactly this, as disadvantaged students likely experience lower rates of summer learning than their more advantaged counterparts and bias their schools' measured quality downward as a result.

There are a number of methods to estimate measures of student achievement growth used in teacher and school accountability models. Though there is hope that the use of more nuanced models can mitigate some of the unintended consequences that arise from using overly simplistic school performance measures (i.e., proficiency rates), concerns remain about potential bias in sophisticated growth models. Researchers have begun to document the sensitivity of growth models to model specification, measurement error, and year-to-year instability.[13] To date, few studies have evaluated whether the summer break poses a validity threat to the use of growth models or inferences about school quality.[14] In a related study, McEachin and Atteberry (2015) provide a technical examination of the role summer plays as a source of bias in one type of growth model: school value-added models. In this chapter, we focus on *student growth percentiles* (SGP), a form of growth model that over half of the states use in their accountability policies.[15] However, while the policy shift toward using growth models in accountability systems improves upon some of the failures of old accountability models, it may not adequately address the bias introduced by the summer learning component of spring-to-spring achievement gains.

SUMMER SETBACK

There is growing evidence that disadvantaged children have fewer learning opportunities during the summer months than their advantaged counterparts. Analyzing a sample of approximately three thousand fifth and sixth graders in Atlanta, Heyns (1978) found that the gap between disadvantaged and advantaged children's test scores grew during the summer faster than in the school year. In a later study of students in Baltimore, Entwisle and Alexander (1992, 1994) found that both socioeconomic and race gaps in reading skills grew at faster rates during the summer. More recently, Downy, Von Hippel, and Broh (2004) found that the socioeconomic and racial/ethnic gaps in reading and math skills are not in fact the product of unequal school systems, but instead are widened primarily during the summer.

More recently, McEachin and Atteberry (2015) also examined the overall patterns of student learning growth from second through ninth grade in the same southern state used in the current analysis. We found statistically significant and policy-relevant variability in students' summer growth rates across all grades, and this differential summer experience contributes meaningfully to the growing disparities in student outcomes that arise during school-age years. In addition, we also found that minority students typically exhibit slower learning rates during summers than their White peers; however, student demographics alone explain little of the variability across students in summer learning rates. This suggests that we do not have good explanations for why certain students lose or gain ground.

Research has suggested that income differences could be related to students' opportunities to practice and learn over summer.[16] For example, Gershenson (2013) found that low-income students watch two more hours of TV per day during the summer than students from wealthier backgrounds.[17] However, Gershenson and Hayes (2014) found that even a rich set of student and family variables explains very little of the differences among students' summer learning patterns. Given that much of students' summer learning is unobserved by the researcher, growth models that conflate the summer period with the school year will inappropriately blame schools with disadvantaged students for this summer loss, and vice versa.[18]

As an example, consider two different hypothetical experiences in figures 2.1 and 2.2 for students who have the same test score in the spring of first and second grade, but differ over the summer. In figure 2.1, the student has a vertically scaled test score of 20 in the spring of first grade and a 30 in the spring of second grade, gaining 10 points over the twelve-month period. We also see that this student did not lose any ground over the summer; in fact, she gained 5 points over the summer, entering the fall of second grade with a score of 25. With the traditional spring-to-spring test timeline, this student's school would

FIGURE 2.1   Example child: Spring scores and one set of missing fall scores

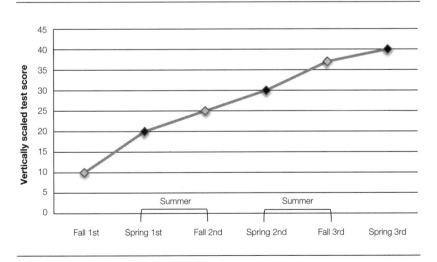

FIGURE 2.2   Example Child: Spring scores and a *different* set of missing fall scores

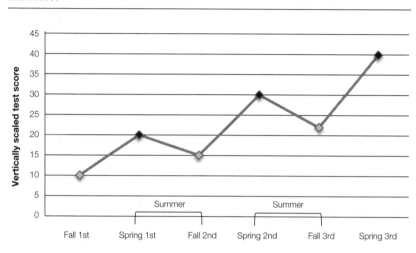

get credited for her 10-point gain in achievement, although only 5 points occurred during the school year. In figure 2.2, the hypothetical student lost 5 points over the summer, falling from a 20 to a 15. However, this same student gained 15 points during second grade, ending the year with a score of 30. With the spring-to-spring test timeline, this school would be credited with 10 points even though the student lost 5 over the summer—out of the school's control—and gained 15 during the school year. If a fall-to-spring test timeline were used instead, the school in figure 2.2 would be labeled more effective than the school in figure 2.1. Given that the trend in figure 2.2, as discussed shortly, is more representative of minority and low-income students, this poses an issue for school accountability policies.

To date, little attention has been paid to the intersection between the summer learning loss literature and growth models, partially due to the ubiquitous spring-to-spring test timeline in education datasets.[19] In his analysis of the sensitivity of teacher value-added scores to different tests, Papay (2011) found that the correlation between teachers' spring-spring and fall-spring value-added scores is between 0.66 and 0.71. Gershenson and Hayes (2014), using data from the Early Childhood Longitudinal Study of 1998–1999 (ELCS), found similar correlations among spring-to-spring and fall-to-spring teacher value-added measures. Lastly, McEachin and Atteberry (2015) and Downy, Von Hippel, and Hughes (2008) conducted school-level analyses and found that larger shares of low-income students were more likely to be in the bottom of the performance distribution when school performance measures do not account for the summer period.

These studies suggest that ignoring the summer vacation will produce a systematic bias in growth models that may also disproportionately affect schools serving larger shares of minority and low-income students under traditional accountability regimes. However, the studies also raise important unanswered questions. The Papay (2011) and Gershenson and Hayes (2014) papers do not investigate the relationship between the spring-to-spring and fall-to-spring value-added discordance and student and school demographics. Downy, Von Hippel, and Hughes (2008), the only study to evaluate this phenomenon at the school level, do not use growth models that are commonly used for school accountability policies or in the education policy literature. The three studies also have important data limitations: they either rely on a few years of data within one urban district, or observe only the summer between kindergarten and first grade for one cohort of nationally representative students.

The results and discussion presented in this chapter address the gaps in the interrelated accountability, growth model, and summer learning literatures in three ways.[20] First, we utilize a statewide panel of student achievement data from grades three through eight over a five-year period. Instead of relying on the summer period between kindergarten and first grade, this study uses a grade span that is more representative of the grades typically included in high-stakes accountability policies. Second, we are the first to evaluate the impact of summer setback on growth models (SGPs) used in state accountability policies and the research literature. Lastly, we examine not only whether summer setback leads to misclassifications in growth models, but also the types of schools that are most affected by this phenomenon.

STUDENT- AND SCHOOL-LEVEL DATA

The data for this study are from the North West Evaluation Association's (NWEA) Measures of Academic Progress (MAP) assessment. The MAP is a computer adaptive test given in math, reading, science, and social studies in over forty US states. To ensure that the MAP scores provide a valid measure of students' knowledge, the NWEA aligns the MAP items with the specific state standards. The MAP is also scored using a vertical and interval scale, which the NWEA calls the RIT scale. The vertical scale allows comparisons of student learning across grades and over time, while the interval scale ensures that a unit increase in a student's score represents the same learning gain across the entire distribution.[21] In sum, the MAP assessment has appropriate measurement properties for a study of school growth models and summer setback.

The data for our study come from a southern state that administered the MAP assessment in the fall and spring for all students in grades two through eight for the 2007–2008 through 2010–2011 school years. We discuss the limitations of using low-stakes assessment data in a later section. Our dataset includes student- and school-level files that are longitudinally matched over time. The student-level file includes basic demographic information, such as the students' race and gender, their math and reading scores, the measurement error associated with their math and reading scores, grade of enrollment, the date of test administration, and fall and spring school IDs. Noticeably, the student-level file does not include indicators for whether the student is an English language learner, belongs to the federal free and reduced-price lunch (FRPL) program, or participates in special education. It is unlikely that the omission of these variables biases our results. As noted earlier, Gershenson and Hayes (2014) find that a rich set of covariates, including detailed socioeconomic data and students' and parents' summer activities, explains only 3 to 5 percent of the variation in students' summer learning, compared to 2.5 percent in our data.

The school-level data file is provided by the Common Core of Data through the NWEA. These data include the typical set of school-level characteristics, including the percent of FRPL students within the school.[22]

STUDENT GROWTH PERCENTILES AND STUDY METHODOLOGY

In this section we present a brief introduction to student growth percentiles (SGPs), which are the most commonly used example of growth models in school accountability systems.[23] SGPs are the conditional median percentile rank of students' current achievement based on their prior achievement histories for a given school. Students are given an SGP of 1 to 99, representing their achievement percentile rank for a given year relative to students with similar achievement histories. A school's SGP is its median student-level SGP. For example, a school with an SGP of 65 indicates that its median student is at the 65th percentile of the conditional current achievement distribution—or, in other words, is performing at least as well as 65 percent of students with the same achievement histories.

While SGPs appear to be a step in the right direction, and an improvement over the achievement level–style accountability under NCLB, their use in school accountability policies rests on two important and strong assumptions: (1) current student, peer, and school inputs do not affect students' achievement; and (2) time-varying and permanent student, family, peer, and school characteristics are captured by the prior achievement histories. In other words, students' prior test scores fully capture all of the possible mechanisms that affected students' past and current achievement, including, but not limited to, the impact of peers, families, and neighborhoods. If this very strong assumption is not met, then SGPs will not do a good job capturing the true effect of schools on students' achievement, and by extension rankings based on SGPs will identify the wrong schools as failing. This is especially true if the SGPs do not capture students' summer learning experiences.[24]

We assess the impact of summer learning loss on schools' SGPs using two models. The first model controls for students' prior spring scores, estimating the effect of schools on students' twelve-month learning (potentially conflating school learning with students' summer learning loss). Second, we add students' fall test scores to the model to account for students' summer learning. In each year, we use as many prior achievements as possible, and we stack the residual from the three years to create one SGP. It is important to note that most states only use the SGP from one year in their accountability models and do not include the off-subject as a control; therefore, our three-year school SGP likely captures the lower bound of the summer loss problem.

RESULTS: EVIDENCE OF POLICY BACKFIRE

We start with a discussion of the correlation between SGPs and student demographics outlined in table 2.1. First, we assess the relationship between schools' average achievement, an NCLB-like measure of school and student demographics. As we have known since the 1960s, the vast majority of student achievement is driven by out-of-school factors (i.e., family wealth, peers, neighborhood quality, and so on). It is not surprising, then, that under NCLB schools serving large shares of minority and low-income students were much more likely to be identified as failing than schools serving White and wealthier students.

TABLE 2.1   The correlation among math and reading growth models and school demographics

	MATH			READING		
		Student growth percentiles			Student growth percentiles	
	Prior spring achievement	Spring to spring	Fall to spring	Prior spring achievement	Spring to spring	Fall to spring
% FRPL	−0.600	−0.274	−0.196	−0.594	−0.427	−0.338
% Minority	−0.558	−0.305	−0.250	−0.549	−0.418	−0.388
Baseline school achievement	0.789	0.352	0.318	0.776	0.399	0.290

We therefore use schools' average achievement levels as a baseline to compare how SGPs fare in mitigating the relationship between proficiency- or achievement level–based school performance measures and student demographics. Consistent with the extant accountability literature, schools' current math and reading achievement is strongly negatively correlated with the share of FRPL and minority students in a school, and strongly positively correlated with schools' prior spring achievement. When we use this status measure of performance as a baseline, spring-to-spring SGPs are an improvement over proficiency or achievement-level accountability models, especially for math. However, the correlation between spring-to-spring reading SGPs and student demographics is still quite negative. This indicates that while the public is sold that the move to using SGPs in accountability systems mitigates many of the problems from the NCLB-era accountability models, this approach is still far from fair. Schools are, in part, held accountable for the types of students they receive, not just how the schools affect student outcomes.

We do see that the movement to a fall-to-spring test timeline greatly diminishes the relationship between student demographics and measures of school quality for math, and moderately improves it for reading. The fall-to-spring math SGP correlations with the share of FRPL and minority students in a school are −0.2 and −0.25, respectively. These lower correlations indicate that high-need schools are nearly as likely to be labeled high performing as wealthier schools. These correlations are likely closer to the true correlation between school quality and demographics that occurs through the teacher labor market. The correlations in table 2.1 show that switching to a fall-to-spring test timeline qualitatively changes the types of schools possibly identified for rewards and/or sanctions under an accountability system, especially for math.

Extant research has documented that growth models used to hold teachers accountable are sensitive to the test timeline (i.e., spring-to-spring versus fall-to-spring).[25] This means that teachers may be labeled as high performing under one test timeline, but not the other. While this discordance is problematic for policy and practice, the research does not differentiate whether the change in the test timeline disproportionally affects certain types of teachers or schools, such as those serving larger shares of traditionally underserved students.

We next provide visual evidence of how the change in test timeline affects the inferences made from school accountability measures. Specifically, we plot schools' math and reading SGPs by tertiles of schools' percentage of FRPL students, shown in figure 2.3. Graphs A and C show the plots of schools' math and reading SGP using a spring-to-spring test timeline, respectively, by the tertiles of the share of FRPL students. If the share of FRPL students in a given school were independent of whether a school was labeled high or low performing, the three separate mounds (the tertiles of FRPL status) would completely overlap. However, we see that in the spring-to-spring test timeline, the top tertile of FRPL (the schools serving the largest share of FRPL students) is to the left of the middle and bottom tertile of FRPL status, indicating that on average schools serving larger shares of FRPL students have lower SGPs than the other two groups. To put this in perspective, the average SGP score for a school serving a

FIGURE 2.3 Plots of schools' spring-to-spring math and reading SGPs

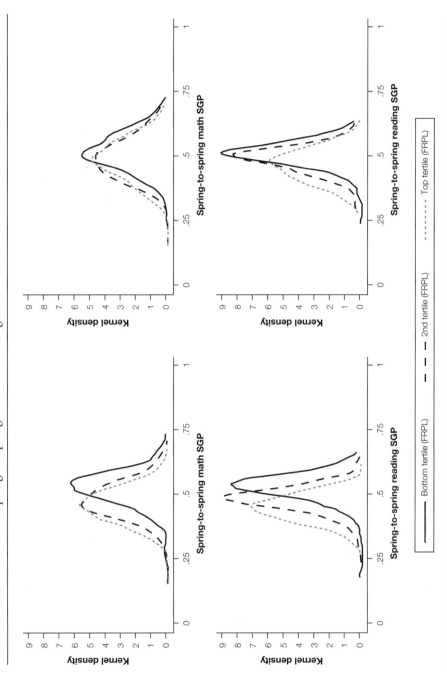

large share of FRPL students is only in the 25th percentile of SGP for schools serving fewer FRPL students.

Graphs B and D show the plots for math and reading SGPs, respectively, for the fall-to-spring test timeline. Removing the summer break from the estimation of schools' math value-add effectively equalizes the distribution of value-add for schools in the middle and top FRPL tertiles. For reading, the average SGP for the top FRPL tertile is now equivalent to approximately the 45th percentile in the bottom FRPL tertile distribution for math and 35th percentile for reading.

Finally, we compare the percent of schools that either move to a higher quintile, stay within the same quintile, or move to a lower quintile of the SGP distribution by FRPL quintiles. The results are presented in table 2.2. Given that we know summer learning loss tends to be worse for minority and low-income students, we would expect schools serving larger shares of these students to do worse in a spring-to-spring test timeline than a fall-to-spring test timeline. We would expect the reverse to be true for wealthier schools. For example, if wealthier students gain ground over the summer, then the aggregation of positive summer experiences for schools serving wealthier students will inflate schools' SGPs. The results in table 2.2 show this exact pattern. Approximately 24 and 31 percent of the schools with the least number of FRPL students are more likely to be in a higher math and reading spring-to-spring SGP quintile than a fall-to-spring quintile, compared to 6 and 9 percent for schools serving the most FRPL students. The opposite pattern occurs when we look at the share of schools that are in a higher fall-to-spring quintile than a spring-to-spring quintile: 3 and 5 percent of the schools serving the least amount of FRPL students are in a higher math fall-to-spring math and reading SGP quintile, compared to 25 and 37 percent for schools serving the most FRPL students. The between-quartile movement is especially problematic for a couple of reasons. First, many states are incorporating an A to F, or similar, grading system for schools in their accountability policies, where the bottom and top 15

TABLE 2.2   The effect of switching test timelines on schools' location in the math and reading SGP distribution

Student growth percentiles

| | MATH | | | | | READING | | | | |
	Bottom quintile of % FRPL students	Q2	Q3	Q4	Top quintile of % FRPL students	Bottom quintile of % FRPL students	Q2	Q3	Q4	Top quintile of % FRPL students
Quintile (spring to spring) > quintile (fall to spring)	24.3%	17.8%	7.9%	7.9%	5.9%	30.9%	31.6%	23.7%	17.1%	8.6%
Quintile (spring to spring) = quintile (fall to spring)	73.0%	77.0%	80.3%	75.0%	69.1%	63.8%	47.4%	52.0%	49.3%	54.6%
Quintile (spring to spring) < quintile (fall to spring)	2.6%	5.3%	11.8%	17.1%	25.0%	5.3%	21.1%	24.3%	33.6%	36.8%

to 20 percent will be identified for sanctions and rewards. Second, extant research suggests that parents are sensitive to the movement of schools across letter grades, as evidenced in donations to public schools and their measures of satisfaction.[26]

AVOIDING BACKFIRE IN ACCOUNTABILITY POLICIES

In an effort to improve upon the shortcomings of using student achievement *levels* to hold schools accountable, the federal government and states have incorporated accountability policies that hold schools accountable for student achievement *growth*, usually determined from the amount of learning between spring assessment periods. The spring-to-spring test timeline includes the three-month summer vacation that students spend away from school. In this chapter we discussed a policy backfire by omitting students' summer learning from measures of school quality in accountability policies. The results have important policy implications.

The first is that while there have been improvements in the design of federal, state, and district school accountability policies, the efficacy of these redesigns is limited by their continued reliance on a spring-to-spring test timeline. The incorporation of a fall test into the typical accountability system mitigates the potential for the summer period to bias school-level growth models. In the case for school SGPs, students' fall achievement serves as a *summer-free* achievement baseline, capturing students' knowledge at the start of the school year. The fall-to-spring test timeline doubles the number of test scores available in students' achievement histories for the SGP model. It allows the researcher to essentially pair students with similar fall *and* spring test scores, instead of relying on just prior spring scores. The move to a fall-to-spring test timeline, along with the move to computer adaptive tests, has the added benefit of providing teachers with information about their students' current achievement levels, and the amount of skills and knowledge lost over the summer.

Although not the main focus of the study, our results build on the literature that evaluates the potential of various growth models, in this case SGPs, to estimate unbiased school effects.[27] The second policy implication is that the SGP approach does not directly account for the impact of student and school differences on student achievement. It assumes that conditional on students' prior achievement histories, schools are equally able to raise the current achievement level of *any* student regardless of his or her background. It is quite straightforward to incorporate student characteristics into the SGP or to use a value-added model that explicitly accounts for student and school differences. Controlling for these characteristics assumes that conditional on students' prior achievement *and other differences that are beyond schools' control*, schools are equally able to raise the current achievement level of their students. Although the SGP assumptions are often more politically palatable, in no case do they have a weaker correlation between student demographics and schools' rankings than other models.[28] The continued use of SGPs to hold schools accountable for student achievement, without adjusting for demographic differences among students and schools, will unfairly punish schools educating traditionally underserved students.

Third, states and districts should use as much data as available when estimating growth models in a high-stakes context. For example, the modal implementation of SGPs estimates a median SGP for a given school in the current year using as many years of prior achievement as are available and does not include the off-subject as a control variable. In results not presented in this chapter, we found that the correlation between student demographics and schools' SGPs was weakest in a fall-to-spring model that included both students' math and reading achievement as control variables. We also found that a spring-to-spring model that used both math and reading achievement as controls was just as effective as a single subject fall-to-spring SGP in mitigating the relationship between demographics and school quality. Furthermore, in this study we pooled data over a number of years to estimate our school-level growth models, a method that potentially smoothed out year-to-year variations in student populations, including students' summer experiences. These changes can be easily implemented for any accountability system, as states are already estimating math and reading school SGPs.

The fourth policy implication is that even when the summer break is removed from our SGPs, there is still a negative correlation between schools' performance and school demographics. It is unclear what the true correlation is between school quality and the schools' political, social, and economic factors, but it is unlikely that it is zero or positive due to labor market preferences, housing preferences, and so on. Furthermore, the relationship between demographics and school quality varies across the growth model used. The results of this study build on nascent extant research to underscore the need for policy makers and educators to first figure out what they want to measure (e.g., school's causal effect on student achievement or a proportional ranking system) before implementing an accountability policy that uses student achievement growth to hold teachers and schools accountable.[29] Regardless of their choice, however, it is unlikely that anything short of a fall-to-spring test timeline will remove the bias from students' summer learning.

The goal of this chapter was to build on the nascent knowledge about the role students' summers play in affecting how we measure school quality in accountability policies. By doing so, we have documented a previously unidentified policy backfire with school accountability policies that hold schools accountable for spring-to-spring student achievement growth. Although accountability policies are implemented to raise overall achievement and close persistent achievement gaps, there's a rich literature about how these policies backfire instead of attaining their stated goals. Students' summer learning is one less discussed source of backfire. In an age of testing and accountability, it is hoped that we can continue to have conversations about how to refine policies that hold educators accountable for student achievement. The good news is that we are in the early stages of a policy backfire with these new accountability systems, and the impending reauthorization of ESEA presents an opportunity for big change. The reauthorization holds the potential to implement lessons learned from the NCLB and waiver backfires in the next round of federal and state accountability policies.

THREE

When Minimum Grading Policies Backfire

Who Decides Whether to Let Students Fail?

Martha Abele Mac Iver

Even though US high school cohort graduation rates are at an all-time high, the failure of a third or more of economically disadvantaged and students of color to meet this minimal requirement for successful entry into the twenty-first-century labor market cannot be ignored. Outcomes for disadvantaged students have improved to some extent over the past two decades, as educational researchers and practitioners have focused considerable attention and effort to transforming the "dropout factories" and equipping schools to intervene with struggling students.[1] But a huge graduation gap, and related opportunity gap, still remains between the classes and the races in American society.

Failure to graduate from high school has many underlying causes, but there is broad research consensus that one of the most critical precipitating factors is course failure, particularly in the ninth grade.[2] Many have argued that much of this failure is preventable, and intervening to help students turn their performance around—before they fail classes and potentially begin a downward spiral to dropping out—makes a great deal of sense.

The question of whether and to what extent districts and schools should be encouraging efforts to prevent course failure has become a political issue. As this chapter will document, there is widespread debate in editorial pages and blogs throughout the country about school district policies that seek to address course failure, and this issue has been the subject of legislative debate and action in Texas. In this chapter I analyze how student failure and efforts to prevent it have become politically charged, and why district policies aimed at quietly helping to reduce student failure have backfired, igniting a raucous public debate and intense opposition. This is a story of how district attempts to implement a policy designed to reduce failure actually increased public opposition to such efforts; more specifically, they created a backlash in public opinion that reinforced the positions of teachers who do not support interventions to prevent course failure. Although efforts to implement the policy and the ensuing backlash may not have *increased* failure rates themselves, they created a political environment around and within schools that proved counterproductive to achieving the intended results. The proliferation of negative opinions about failure prevention in the media certainly increased in the wake of district policy efforts and the publicity surrounding them. After recounting this policy story, I offer some reflections about how the current "politics of failure" might be reframed in a way that leads to more nuanced discussion of different types of failure and their impact on students and society. Taking time to discuss the issues surrounding failure more systematically, and to build a broader consensus among teachers about how grading fits into the larger goals they are seeking to achieve, is essential as we seek to prepare students for productive lives in the twenty-first century.

MINIMUM GRADING: ORIGINS OF THE POLICY AND THE ENSUING DEBATE

District leaders who understand the research on factors influencing graduation rates recognize the importance of reducing the high school course failure rate (since graduation is linked to passing courses to earn required credits). As several education researchers have noted over the past couple of decades, students often fail courses because they accumulate zeros for uncompleted assignments, and it becomes statistically impossible for them to achieve a passing grade of 60 (or 70, where some schools and districts have set the passing cutoff) when even a few zeros are averaged together. Policy arguments have been made regarding how to adjust the statistical impact of zeros so that students have opportunities to recover from early failure and pass courses.[3] One proposed policy treats the grading scale as a 50- to 100-point scale (corresponding to the 0.0 to 4.0 scale) that eliminates the numerically small versions of the F grade (grades below 50) that prevent so many students from recovering from failure. For example, if a course grade is based on five equally weighted papers and a student receives a 0 for the first two because the papers were not submitted on time, even grades of 90 on the last three papers will yield an average grade of 54 (failing) on the 100-point scale; on a 4-point scale the average is a passing grade of 2.1 (C)—even if 90s are treated as 3.5 and 0s as 0s. Advocates have defended this minimum grading policy empirically against criticisms of lowered standards and social promotion.[4]

In response to this widespread discussion among educators, many schools and districts that use a 100-point scale began mandating a "no grade lower than 50" policy. This simple formula would assign all students with any failing mark a grade of 50 in systems using a numerical scale. As just noted, this is mathematically equivalent to using an A-to-F scale ranging from 4 to 0—the typical "four-point" grading scale. Students who continued to receive failing grades would fail the course, but those who made significant efforts to improve would have a statistical chance of passing it.

On the surface, implementation of such a policy should theoretically increase course-passing rates if failures are often triggered by students perceiving failure as inevitable after a certain point in the year. But when such a policy triggers public opposition, the backlash can strengthen teachers' commitment to teaching students "responsibility" by enforcing traditional grading policies that do not offer opportunities to recover from failure. Although such opposition to the policy may not increase failure rates per se, the increase in negative public discourse creates a more negative environment among faculties in high schools as they confront the issues associated with student success. Public debate on this policy began to increase exponentially following the publication of a *USA Today* article, entitled "At Some Schools, Failure Goes from Zero to 50," in May 2008.[5] The article was featured the next week in the Principal's Update from the National Association of Secondary School Principals, along with an invitation to "Take the Principal's Poll: Should Schools Adopt Policies to Raise the Minimum Grade from Zero to 50?"[6] Principals voted and bloggers slugged it out on the Web.[7] What was meant to be a quiet, administrative way to help students recover from failure was going viral.

By 2009 the Texas Classroom Teacher Association (TCTA) was debating this issue at its annual convention and working with a state senator to draft legislation prohibiting minimum grading policies. A locally focused policy had been blown up to the state level and politicized beyond imagination. As TCTA described its role, "Education Commissioner Robert Scott informally polled TCTA members at the February [2009] annual convention and was surprised at the number of participants who indicated they could be required to assign a minimum grade under local policies." TCTA subsequently provided draft bill language and collaborated with [Senator Jane] Nelson on the bill.[8] An April 2009 news release from the office of Senator Nelson, a former sixth-grade teacher, quoted the Education Commissioner's testimony before the Senate Nominations Committee, in which he said, "I recently asked teachers attending a conference how many were barred from giving low grades. I was stunned when half of the hands went up."[9] Another news release quoted the senator's rationale for her bill about "no-fail grading": "Students will live up to the expectations we set for them. Minimum grade policies reward minimum effort. Teachers are in the best position to judge a student's work and should have the freedom to assign grades that reflect the merit of a student's performance."[10]

The wording of Senate Bill (SB) 2033 was relatively simple:

> A school district shall adopt a grading policy, including provisions for the assignment of grades on class assignments and examinations, before each school year. A district grading policy: (1) must require a classroom teacher to assign a grade that reflects the student's relative mastery of an assignment; (2) may not require a classroom teacher to assign a minimum grade for an assignment without regard to the student's quality of work; and (3) may allow a student a reasonable opportunity to make up or redo a class assignment or examination for which the student received a failing grade.[11]

The bill passed unanimously in both the Texas Senate and House in April and May of 2009 and went into effect immediately. Local school grading policies were now governed by state legislation.

Because the wording of the bill referred to assignments and examinations, some Texas districts complied with the letter of the law but still required that failing marking period grades be recorded as 50 on report cards. Local administration of grading policies had to be micromanaged by the state education agency. The state education commissioner sent a letter to district administrators in October 2009 to clarify the agency's interpretation of the legislation:

> [Texas Education Agency] understands this legislation to also require honest grades for each grading period including six weeks, nine weeks, or semester grades for two reasons. First, if actual grades on assignments are not used in determining a six weeks grade, the purpose of the legislation has been defeated. Second, since 1995, Texas Education Code, §28.021, has

required decisions on promotion or course credit to be based
on "academic achievement or demonstrated proficiency." If the
six weeks grades do not reflect the actual assignment grades,
they would not reflect academic achievement or demonstrated
proficiency.[12]

By November 2009 several districts in the Houston area had filed
a lawsuit challenging the commissioner's interpretation of the legislation. One of the districts asserted that its policy of a minimum
grade of 50 on the quarterly report card had been in place for twenty
years and that the state was infringing on local control by mandating
grading practices.[13] The public debate continued while the case was
awaiting a decision. In a November 2009 press release Senator Nelson
declared: "It is a sad state of affairs when school districts are willing
to go to court for the right to force their teachers to assign fraudulent
grades. When I filed this bill, many were skeptical as to whether these
policies even existed in our schools. Now we know the truth—that
administrators are substituting their judgment for that of our teachers in the classroom. Not only that, they are willing to waste precious
education resources on a misguided lawsuit to continue these policies,
which undermine the authority of our teachers and reward minimum
effort from students."[14] The Texas Classroom Teachers Association
weighed in again in March 2010: "TCTA considers this an important issue of teacher authority in the classroom, and we will continue
the fight for proper implementation of a law that the Legislature intended districts to abide by. TCTA members in a district that has continued some version of a minimum grading policy should contact the
TCTA Legal Department."[15] A judge ruled against the districts in June
2010, and they decided not to appeal. The Texas branch of the American Federation of Teachers applauded the decision in August 2010
with the headline: "As School Year Starts, Teachers' Grading Authority Bolstered."[16] In 2011 Senator Nelson sponsored a subsequent bill,

SB 79, aimed at clarifying the language of SB 2033 and codifying the judge's ruling. As Nelson put it: "This bill is intended to ensure that Texas school districts may not require teachers to artificially inflate a student's grade, including report card grades or other cumulative grade averages."[17] And so the good intention of Texas districts to quietly implement a policy aimed at helping students recover from early failure backfired: it succeeded in alienating teachers and the public to such an extent that politicians intervened and legislated against their efforts to prevent failure.

A systematic analysis of the impact of this legislation on Texas ninth-grade course-passing (i.e., on track to graduation) rates is beyond the scope of this chapter (as the data were not available to the author), but data from the Dallas Independent School District (ISD) are illustrative of subsequent high school course-failure rates in the years following the legislation. Dallas ISD has been producing reports on its ninth-grade on-track indicator, a measure based on the number of credits earned during ninth grade and the number of semester failures in core subjects, since the 2007–2008 school year. Its 2014 report summarized trends since 2008–2009, noting that the on-track rate dropped in 2009–2010 and has varied only slightly since then, with fewer than three-quarters (72 percent in 2013–2014) of non-magnet-school ninth graders on track to graduation.[18] While it is not clear that the legislation itself was responsible for the decline in on-track rates for Dallas students in 2009–2010, it is clear that the goal of increasing the proportion of students on track to graduation has not been realized.

WHY DID DISTRICT EFFORTS TO SUPPORT HIGH SCHOOL STUDENT SUCCESS BACKFIRE?

Even if minimum grading policies were associated with only failing to improve student on-track rates—and not necessarily with increasing the failure rates they were designed to decrease—we can interpret the politicization of minimum grading in Texas and throughout the editorial pages nationwide as a backfire. District attempts to solve an issue administratively and quietly, bypassing discussions with teachers that could become emotional and divisive, succeeded in generating much more heated debate and opposition at the state political level. One could say that the attempt to bypass the micropolitics of dialogue at the schoolhouse town meeting backfired by catapulting the issue to the state house, where discussion was dominated by sound bites and ideological pronouncements, and a counterpolicy was mandated by legislation. Seeking to implement a policy administratively and avoid contentious debate among teachers within their schools backfired for districts, resulting in an even more politicized and ideological attack on their efforts to help students recover from failure and succeed in school.

Analysis of the rhetoric in the public opposition to minimum grading in Texas identifies three major themes that resonate widely in American public opinion and help to explain how the issue became politicized and district policies backfired. These district policies were viewed as a threat both to teacher autonomy and to incentivizing students to work hard in school. And the issue was framed in moral terms that characterized minimum grading policies as fraudulent and deceitful and the legislation as "truth in grading." Next I examine each of these rhetorical themes more fully to explain why district efforts alienated their stakeholder publics and therefore backfired.

A Threat to Teacher Authority and Autonomy

Teachers and their supporters in the state legislative houses viewed district policies on minimum grading as a direct challenge to teacher authority and autonomy in assigning student grades. Press releases and media commentary criticized district actions for undermining teacher authority and professional judgment. Grading has been traditionally associated with teacher autonomy and regarded as "sacred ground."[19] As Cox points out, "grades and grading remain largely the domain of individual teachers, particularly at the secondary level" despite all the recent standards-based curricular reforms.[20] Orders from principals to teachers, such as "You're going to have to change all of the failing grades to passing," have evoked teacher fury in blog after blog.[21]

Teacher autonomy in assigning grades has even become a constitutional issue since the Texas legislation was passed. A teacher in Louisiana who was instructed by her principal not to give any grade lower than 60 to her fourth graders brought a lawsuit against the school district in 2010, charging that this violated her First Amendment rights. A district court concurred with the teacher's claim that assigning failing grades was "protected speech" under the First Amendment.[22] This judicial decision underscores the societal consensus around teacher autonomy in grading practices.

A Failure to Build Responsibility and Work Ethic in Students

The policy on minimum grading also violated teachers' (and the wider public's) sense of duty to build responsibility in adolescent students. Opponents of minimum grading believe that creating systems that allow recovery from failure will encourage students to do even less work than they would under a system that would average all zeros for missing work into a final course grade. In their view, continuing to provide "second chances" to students sends entirely the wrong message about workplace requirements and deadlines. They do not want to encourage the kind of work ethic that would result in graduates getting fired in the workplace. They associate "minimum grades" with "minimum effort." As a commentator on a Tennessee district's recent decision to implement a similar minimum grading policy put it: "You're letting kids know exactly that they have to do the bare minimum to achieve a passing grade and that's ridiculous . . . It doesn't teach them that there are consequences for failure and there are consequences for not producing hard work."[23]

Underlying this commitment to building student responsibility is the widespread entrepreneurial culture in the United States that celebrates the importance of learning from failure.[24] As an entrepreneur recently quoted by the *Economist* explained, "The biggest difference between America and Europe is that European investors won't touch you if you have a failed business behind you. In America they won't touch you unless you have. If there is one thing that distinguishes the most creative, entrepreneurial economies it is this embracing of failure, the idea that, in Henry Ford's words, 'failure is simply the opportunity to begin again, this time more intelligently.'"[25] The entrepreneurial world's emphasis on the importance of learning from failure has influenced educational thinking as well. The *Guardian* recently highlighted a British teacher's argument about "why Olympians and A-level students all need to fail," and Paul Tough echoed those themes in his *New York Times Magazine* essay "What If the Key to Success Is Failure?"[26] Those who hold this view believe that people who haven't confronted failure at an earlier age and learned to overcome it are often the ones who fall apart psychologically when it finally arrives. They argue that allowing children and adolescents to fail and to learn about recovering from failure is a crucial part of development.

A Moral Framing of the Issue

The framing of the issue as "truth in grading" also reflects a cultural divide. Policies that recoded any average score below 50 on the 100-point scale to a 50 were thus characterized as fraudulent. As one recent blogger has put it: "Minimum grades are lies."[27] The unchallenged assumption behind all the rhetoric was the absolute nature of the 100-point grading scale. One cannot help but wonder why districts did not seek to institute letter grading, linked to the four-point scale (with Fs calculated as a 0 and A's as a 4). Such a grading system, common in many districts, achieves exactly the same goal as the minimum grading policy without any semblance of teacher coercion, wrongful incentives to students, or fraud. Why is the 100-point scale so deeply entrenched in the American experience (especially in the one society that has avoided using the metric system)? That is one mystery that deserves time for exploration.

MOVING FROM TOP-DOWN MANDATED POLICIES TO BUILDING CONSENSUS

As this case study from Texas illustrates, district efforts to address the problem of student failure through authoritarian policy decrees are probably doomed to fail. Widely held philosophies among teachers and the general public are deeply entrenched and resistant to bureaucratic decrees. Mandates from administrators to teachers, such as a policy of "no grade lower than 50," neither engage teachers in a collaborative discussion aimed at persuading them to examine their practice and its effects nor equip them with strategies for motivating students to change their behaviors.[28]

Attempts at reform to help struggling students backfired, at least in part, because policy makers neglected to spend more time engaging in dialogue with teachers about how to address student motivation issues and the ramifications of failure on high-stakes, universally required tasks. Even more important is making time for school staff to discuss different types of failure and the ramifications of each for individuals and society—a topic developed more fully in a moment. Because time to engage in these types of discussions is extremely limited within most schools and districts, it is not surprising that districts seek to solve issues like high rates of student failure through administrative decrees and policy decisions. But failure to engage in the process of dialogue and consensus building often results in failure to achieve the desired results. Next I propose a framework for thinking about failure that could structure these kinds of critical discussions between schools and districts and their broader constituencies and stakeholder groups.

A TYPOLOGY TO PROMOTE DIALOGUE ON DIFFERENTIATED RESPONSES TO DIFFERENT TYPES OF FAILURE

Schools as professional learning communities need to explore more systematically how we might think about failure and its implications. I propose a simple typology that I suspect frames many people's thinking about failure, even though I have not found it written down anywhere explicitly. Making this framework explicit can help guide conversations by differentiating types of failure and their effects. These conversations can potentially help to build consensus among school faculties and the mass public regarding the meaning of failure in different contexts and the overarching goals for the grading systems that have such an impact on students' lives and futures.

Let's distinguish failure along two dimensions in this typology: what kind of task versus how much is at stake. We can divide tasks into two basic categories: universal requirements versus optional skills or selective groupings. *Universal requirements* are those for which everyone needs to meet a certain minimal standard to function successfully in society at a basic level. *Optional skills or selective groupings* are not necessary or even possible for everyone to attain. And we can characterize the level of the stakes as low versus high. *Low stakes* are associated with formative opportunities for feedback with few if any lasting ramifications, while *high stakes* implies a summative assessment that carries lasting consequences. Table 3.1 summarizes this typology of failure and gives some illustrative examples.

Some tasks are really universal requirements for normal life in society, such as the need to learn to read and to meet standards for receiving a high school diploma. Other tasks are nonuniversal, such as meeting standards in music, art, or sports. By definition, achieving at a superior level in order to meet selective criteria for an elite group (cast of a play, a sports team, a selective school or college, etc.) is a nonuniversal requirement. Demonstrating mastery of particular

TABLE 3.1   Failure typology with illustrative examples

		STAKES LEVEL	
		Low (formative)	High (summative)
Task category	Universal requirements • K–12 grade-level achievement standards • High school diploma • High school exit exams	• Homework • Classwork • Interim assessments	• K–8 promotion criteria • Final high school course grades • High school exit exam
	Optional skills or selective groupings • Music, art, drama, sports • Entry into selective high school or college • College-level gate-keeper course to higher-level courses • Entry into graduate/ professional school	• Practice sessions • Practice work • Interim assessments	• Auditions/tryouts • AP credit • Admissions decision • GRE scores • College course grades

academic subjects at the college level or achieving success in particular professional pursuits would also be considered nonuniversal standards. Not everyone needs to pass College Chemistry 101. And not everyone needs to start a successful business enterprise or work as a doctor or lawyer.

It is also important to differentiate between stake levels in evaluating task mastery. In the language of assessment, one needs to distinguish between a series of low-stakes formative assessments and a final, high-stakes summative assessment. This involves clarifying a timeframe and process for assessing mastery that encourages individuals to persevere. One can think of this as a way of framing conditions that allow individuals to follow the old maxim, "If at first you don't succeed, try, try again." When individuals are first learning a skill, we expect that mastery will take time. Toddlers fall again and again as they are learning to walk. Novice readers make mistakes. Budding pianists hit lots of wrong notes. Students learning math often get their first practice problems wrong. We need to establish a time period during which failure to do the task correctly is like a toddler's fall: one must simply get up and try it again without any real penalties. Students need a low-stakes formative period for practicing (in classwork and homework and taking interim assessments) that simply allows them to see the need for more practice. Treating almost all assessment as formative (giving feedback for how to improve, without penalty or labeling of "failure") is crucial for the learning process.

One can see that experiences of failure are to be expected as normal in three of the four stakes-level quadrants in the failure typology I have proposed. The common argument about the importance of helping students learn to cope with failure fits extremely well within the bottom two stakes-level quadrants of nonuniversal requirements. After a period of practice and feedback, not making the team or the cast for the school play is an appropriate way to learn about coping with failure. Not everyone can make the cut. Even the experience of not succeeding at first on formative assessments around a required or universal standard is an important lesson learned by most students at some point. When the stakes are low, with no penalties, students have the freedom to learn from mistakes and persevere toward mastery of the standards.

The problem arises when failure rates rise above a negligible level for high-stakes summative assessments of universal requirements (the shaded area of table 3.1). When students are failing in K–12 coursework that is considered mandatory in our society, it is essential for schools to probe more deeply to understand and address the reasons for this failure, rather than simply communicating it to students and parents on a report card. Assigning a failing grade in such a case resembles the bureaucratic top-down mandate: because we are pressed for time we fail to discuss crucial issues, instead substituting an authoritative *diktat* that does not even achieve its ostensible goals. Receiving a summative assessment of failure at the end of a required course rarely motivates students to try harder to be successful. High-stakes failure on universally required tasks often leads more to discouragement and a downward academic spiral than to inspiration to persevere and fight one's way back. Even failure on interim high-stakes assessments, such as high school course grades, has counterproductive effects on students' futures. Research in district after district has clearly shown that a pattern of course failure in ninth grade is linked to increasing disengagement with school, through lower rates of attendance that often culminate in dropout.[29] The probability of high school graduation declines substantially with each ninth-grade course failure. Other research suggests that early encounters with school failure become a self-fulfilling prophecy for struggling students.[30] Failure is not the same kind of motivator for these students as it was for inventors like Henry Ford; school failure is a qualitatively different type of failure.

When students fail on high-stakes assessments of universally required standards (such as high school courses required for graduation), a systemic alert must sound and the system must respond to both understand the causes of failure and plan how to prevent it in the future. As Stringfield and others have argued regarding schools as high-reliability organizations, "both the public and the professional educators must realize that in the 21st century the costs of educational failure are catastrophic for the individual students who do not achieve their full potential and for the rest of us in society . . . There must be a perception existing, or created early on, that failure to achieve core goals is unacceptable."[31] How do we build consensus among teachers and the American public regarding the necessity of creating structures and systems that ensure that students succeed in meeting minimal standards?

AVOIDING BACKFIRE IN MINIMUM GRADING POLICIES

Addressing the problem of student failure to meet minimal educational standards for the twenty-first century requires a new approach.

Top-down administrative decrees have not succeeded. We need to take the time to engage in dialogue and persuasion to change deeply held beliefs about teacher autonomy in grading and how to effectively build responsibility in adolescents (not to mention irrational convictions about the absolute nature of the 100-point scale). The Center for Social Organization of Schools at Johns Hopkins University School of Education is taking up this challenge in a new project funded by the Institute for Education Sciences. Working with teachers at a couple of urban high schools with high course failure rates, we are developing a series of interactive professional development modules that include teacher debates and other creative means of fostering dialogue among teachers about how to motivate students to do what it takes to be successful in their courses. This work will help teachers foster the development of student responsibility in productive ways that focus on getting work done rather than just penalizing students for not doing it. And it will help to increase the sense of collective responsibility for student learning that is so strongly linked to positive student outcomes.[32] We believe that collaborative dialogue will persuade teachers—like the one who cheerfully told me recently that she gave a zero to a student who had not done the assignment because he turned in only one paragraph for the five-paragraph essay—that their goal is to move struggling students toward success rather than to brand them as failures. In a recent presentation of this work I faced a roomful of instructional coaches and facilitators who all confessed that they had once been that teacher who failed students without flinching. It *is* possible to change teacher attitudes and practice. But it will take dialogue and persuasion. It will take time. Devoting time for teachers to collaboratively learn about what it takes to motivate struggling students and help them succeed will save the much greater time required for credit recovery and dropout reengagement. It will be time well spent.

FOUR

When School Closures Backfire

What Happened to the Students at Jefferson High School?

Matthew N. Gaertner, Ben Kirshner,
and Kristen M. Pozzoboni

Of all the accountability sanctions public schools face, closure is probably the most severe. If, after years of inadequate growth in student achievement, a school remains unable to produce expected levels of academic proficiency, it may be shut down. This should not be confused with *reconstitution*, whereby school leaders and faculty members are released or reassigned, and replaced by new staff. Closure is a more drastic remedy; not only are school staff sent elsewhere, but the building is either closed or given over to be used by charter management organizations.

The theory of action may be intuitive—educational environments that have become toxic and unproductive should be significantly reshuffled, if not abandoned entirely. The students who move out should, the argument goes, be able to regain their academic footing in more nurturing and rigorous school settings. There are just a few problems with this logic. First, it is a theory of action that was deployed widely before it was tested empirically. "Best practices" in school closure have therefore been developed on the fly, as researchers and practitioners learn from past missteps. Second, it does not acknowledge that there are often not significantly better alternatives, particularly if one weighs the alternatives against hardships associated with closure, such as longer transportation times and navigating new social environments. Third, closures disproportionately affect communities of color and typically disregard the rights of parents and neighborhood residents to have a voice in decision making about their school. Finally, the measures by which schools have been identified for closure are limited, focusing on relatively narrow domains of academic achievement (for example, mathematics and reading scores on standardized tests).

We recognize the value of standardized tests for monitoring student progress. We will, in fact, discuss assessment results at some length in the pages to come. But limiting school closure narratives to stories about test score trends—to the exclusion of just about everything else—shortchanges what should be a robust and inclusive democratic decision-making process. School closures may be triggered by the calculus of academic achievement, but they impact families and communities. Failing to anticipate those impacts can lead well-intentioned policies to backfire. Refining the school closure theory of action therefore will require broadening the ways closure decisions are made and closure effects are assessed.

In this chapter's analysis of a school closure, we will attempt to honor both sets of criteria: achievement indicators such as test scores, dropout rates, and graduation rates, and more nuanced features of student experiences related to the challenges imposed by closure. Our narrative structure reflects our central conclusions: We home in on academic outcomes because we believe school environments (and disruptions in those environments) will affect achievement. We home in on student voices because, perhaps obviously, understanding the impact of a school closure requires understanding the experiences of the students it has displaced.[1]

There are, of course, many phases to any school closure—the years prior, when dwindling attendance or stagnant test scores stoke public concern; the years during, when the school closes its doors and students and staff transition to new buildings; and the years after, when some closed schools reopen following a hiatus, reborn for a new cohort. In this chapter we focus on the years during. In doing so, we do not mean to trivialize the antecedents of a closure, nor the potential long-term benefits of hard-nosed accountability policy for all public schools. But even if there is a strong utilitarian argument behind accountability sanctions like school closure, education policy should be guided by a fairly simple principle: "First, do no harm." Or, in the spirit of this volume, "Don't backfire." Gauging policy backfire means examining the lives of the students directly impacted. In our case, these students comprised the graduating classes of 2006 through 2010 at Jefferson High School. We pick up their story in early 2006.

THE CLOSURE YEAR: 2005–2006

On February 15, the Riverside school board voted to close Jefferson High School. The decision was to take effect that spring. Graduating seniors would finish their high school careers at Jefferson, but the school's ninth-, tenth-, and eleventh-grade students were displaced— in other words, instructed to transfer to other schools in the district to complete high school.

In the years preceding the closure, Jefferson's enrollment had been shrinking (by 47 percent since 2002), and the school had been repeatedly rated unsatisfactory based on results from state achievement tests. In 2005, fewer than 6 percent of its students were proficient in math and fewer than 9 percent were proficient in writing. In light of Jefferson's waning population and its students' academic struggles, the Riverside School District (RSD) publicly touted the closure as a "rescue mission": displaced students would have the opportunity to relocate to higher performing schools and would therefore stand a better chance of progressing academically and graduating on time.

It was roughly at this point that our involvement in the project began. A youth organizing group contacted Ben (the second author of this chapter) and expressed an interest in conducting a study of the closure's impact.[2] The analyses were modest to start, beginning with documentation of the closure announcement itself and subsequent reactions. In the summer of 2006 the project quickly expanded to include both in-depth qualitative research studies (including student interviews, focus groups, and open-ended surveys) and longitudinal quantitative analyses of displaced students' academic outcomes (including test score trends, graduation rates, and dropout rates).

Throughout this chapter we will draw upon findings from those qualitative and quantitative studies, but we will avoid the "literature review/methods/findings/discussion" orthodoxy typical of academic manuscripts. Rather, we will highlight quantitative results and student narratives as appropriate, as the story of the closure progresses—just as we believe quantitative trends and student voice should be heeded in equal measure during high-impact educational decision-making processes. With that bit of structural and methodological housekeeping out of the way, we return to the closure announcement.

Jefferson's History

To understand how the closure announcement was received by the Jefferson community, it is important to know a bit about the history of the school and its district (all names are pseudonyms to respect confidentiality agreements). Riverside is a large, urban school district in the western United States. Like many urban districts, RSD has experienced substantial demographic shifts over the past three decades and an increase in racial and socioeconomic segregation. The problem of segregation was exacerbated in the 1990s when White flight and an end to interdistrict busing policies isolated low-income Latino and African American students in the Riverside school system. Despite

reforms (including districtwide school choice policies and the rede-
sign of some comprehensive high schools into smaller learning academies), RSD has struggled to create and sustain integrated schools and
narrow persistent racial and economic gaps in educational attainment.

Within RSD, Jefferson High School was an institution that had
served a historically African American community for more than
a century. The school was known for both quality academic offerings and a strong vocational program. Near the end of the busing era,
there were as many White students at Jefferson as there were Black
students, and only about a quarter of the students were eligible for
free or reduced-price lunch (FRPL). That changed in 1996, when the
end of court-ordered busing quickly and radically altered Jefferson's
demographic profile. By 2006, 2 percent of Jefferson students were
White, and 92 percent were FRPL-eligible. Trends in student achievement followed suit, and despite a number of short-lived reform efforts, by 2005 Jefferson's schoolwide accountability rating was the
lowest among RSD's high schools.[3]

Concerned about academic trends at Jefferson and limited district resources to support the success of its students, RSD officials
held meetings in early 2006 to discuss the school's future.[4] Students
and parents were reportedly assured an outright closure was not on
the table, but much to the community's surprise, the school board decided Jefferson would shut its doors at the end of the 2005–2006 academic year.[5]

The Immediate Aftermath: Student Voices

Jefferson students and the surrounding community were upset by
the decision, and perplexed by how it could have come with so little warning. The frustration played out on multiple dimensions.
First, although the Riverside school board assured students the decision was made for their benefit, community members felt the closure would cause more problems than it would solve. One student
attending the school board meeting put it more eloquently: "You're

putting barriers in front of us instead of removing 'em." Another student lamented in an interview, "They're making it harder; they're just making it harder."

Second, given Jefferson's history as a cornerstone of the city's African American community and its recent and rapid resegregation, it was difficult for some to see the closure as anything other than an attack on Black and brown students. In some cases students felt they were being blamed for the closure; one noted, "It's just kinda how students took it. 'Oh, you're going to close our school, so that must mean that we're bad and . . . we weren't doing our jobs and we're stupid and our scores are so low.'" Other students drew sharp contrasts between accountability sanctions against schools in poorer city neighborhoods and expansions in wealthier ones: "It is difficult to look at the eight schools in Southeast Riverside that are struggling without comparing them to the two brand-new elementary schools being built a mile away in the shiny new Woodside development."

Finally—and most apropos of this chapter's policy prescriptions—students felt they did not have sufficient input into the decision. As one succinctly put it, "I don't think that there was . . . any consideration for anyone. It was just like they decided to close it and there was nothing that the community could have did or said." Indeed, focus group, interview, and student survey results suggested that (1) few students felt they had participated adequately in closure deliberations, and (2) students did not want to take a passive role in deciding Jefferson High School's future.

Even a full year after the closure—when presumably the initial sting would have worn off and new schools would seem more like home—students expressed bitterness about the decision. "It was unfair to shut down Jefferson—it didn't help Jefferson's problems, it only made them worse," "They locked us out with no remorse," and "They didn't care about how the students feel over this!" were just a few of the criticisms collected through retrospective surveys.

The Immediate Aftermath: Test Score Trends

After the closure decision in February, statewide standardized tests loomed. At the time, RSD tested all middle school, ninth-grade, and tenth-grade students in reading and mathematics each year. Historically, Jefferson students' scores would go up over time as they progressed through middle school and high school.[6] That ended after the closure. In fact, scores dropped rather precipitously for the ninth and tenth graders who took the statewide tests in spring 2006.

To better operationalize "precipitously," let us contextualize score trends by defining a year's worth of growth for the typical Jefferson student—a racial minority (that is, Black or Latino) eligible for FRPL. From 2003 to 2005, between sixth grade and tenth grade, these Jefferson students on average grew about 20 points per year in math and 19 points in reading, and those trends were fairly linear.[7] In 2006, after the closure announcement, Jefferson students on average dropped 3 points in math and 16 points in reading—that is 0.15 and 0.84 years' worth of decline for math and reading, respectively. In the language of longitudinal analysis, the closure announcement introduced a "discontinuity" in displaced students' standardized test score trends.[8] In the language of one Jefferson student surveyed a year after the closure, "The district screwed us over."

Of course, it is fair to argue that Jefferson students could not possibly have lost nearly a year's worth of knowledge and skills in any subject area in the few months that passed between the closure announcement and testing day. Steep declines in test scores could reasonably be cast as Jefferson students protesting the test-based accountability policies that contributed to the school's closure. A temporary drop in test scores does not prove that educational harm has been done. So did this policy produce effects that were counter to RSD's intentions? Did the closure backfire? The better test would be students' experiences and academic outcomes the following year, when they left Jefferson and enrolled in new high schools.

THE TRANSITION YEAR: 2006–2007

The 374 displaced students who stayed in RSD following Jefferson's closure enrolled in 23 separate schools across RSD. Most, however (70 percent), enrolled in one of four large comprehensive high schools in the district. This transition, as one might expect, disrupted Jefferson students' familiar academic routines and school connections. Some of the challenges students faced were more immediate (such as finding new friends and maintaining old friendships disrupted by the closure) and some built slowly (such as handling new academic demands and establishing meaningful relationships with the new schools' staff). Each new challenge reflects a different aspect of the closure experience for impacted students, and each illustrates an opportunity for districts to better manage school closures in the future, so we will parse the next few pages according to these topics.

Relationships

If changing schools is never easy, making the transition during the teenage years may be particularly hard. This is true not only because many teenagers form tight friendship bonds with their schoolmates, but also because they have started to establish trusting relationships with adults at the school—teachers, staff, and leadership. Students who left Jefferson for new destinations in fall 2006 found that both types of relationships were disrupted by the closure. One student noted in an interview that seeing "my teachers go to other schools" made it "difficult to start all over at the new school." Through a survey, another said, "I still don't want to be here. I wish I could be at Jefferson where I got along with more people."

One might assume that in a putatively failing school like Jefferson, relationships between staff and students would have been weak, or even worse, antagonistic. But students in our qualitative sample reported the opposite. Many indicated that Jefferson, despite its problems, was like family. "At Jefferson," one survey respondent noted, "I felt like I was at home. I felt like the staff really did care about us and our education."

Familial trust fostered not only a sense of belonging at Jefferson, but also (at least in students' eyes) individualized academic attention. This was a theme that pervaded our qualitative results. Survey respondents said, "At Jefferson they actually cared about what you learned" and "teachers wanted them to be in school." The level of positive regard for Jefferson should not be understated; none of the survey respondents expressed negative views about adults at the school, and as one student noted, "I loved my teachers at Jefferson. I trust them for everything."

Relationships like those that existed between Jefferson students and staff take time to build, so it is not surprising that many displaced students (40 percent of survey respondents) said they struggled to form similarly close bonds in their new schools. Although many of the interview participants and survey respondents said there was at least one adult at their new schools that treated them fairly (respondents also used words like "nice," "respectful," and "good"), many students in the qualitative study voiced serious frustrations about their new-school experience. As one student wrote, "It is way different because at Jefferson I had relationships w/ my teachers and here I really don't." Another student's comment crystallized how a generally respectful atmosphere at the new schools did not necessarily translate to individualized support: "As far as I can see, some of the teachers that I know are nice to me and treat me good, but the thing is they don't care if you pass their class."

Finally, although a large contingent of displaced students landed in respectful and fair environments after leaving Jefferson, some felt stigmatized. In reporting their experiences we do not mean to overemphasize mentions of "stereotyping" in the data (only a quarter of displaced students brought it up), but some students' reflections are worth mentioning. One respondent wrote, "People label us as bad, stupid, or useless but people don't know what it feels like to be forced out and no one will ever understand the struggles we face every day." Another stated that youth and adults at his new school "are always thinking that we are dumb and every time one student does something wrong they always say that that's why they closed Jefferson."

These patterns are not unique to our research; others have found, for example, that teachers fear displaced students will bring aggregate test scores down at their new schools.[9] Such fears may not be unwarranted; displaced students usually arrive from lower performing schools, and will face quite a few academic challenges in their new environments.

We will turn to academic challenges next, but before we do it is fair to point out that displaced students' criticisms of their new school environments may reflect a need to come to Jefferson's defense. Some students may have touted their old school's strengths to counter the negative messages implied by the closure. It is also fair to point out that RSD knew its decision to close Jefferson would be difficult for students and tried to improvise some supports, including providing free buses to some schools and setting students up with mentors. In that light we should gauge the closure's effects according to its architects' designs. If displaced students eventually settled in and succeeded in their new schools, the closure could be deemed a wise, albeit momentarily painful, policy decision. Academic declines helped seal Jefferson's fate. With the closure behind them, would displaced students' academic fortunes be reversed? Our analysis of test scores, dropout, and graduation suggest the answer is no.

Academics: Test Score Trends

Recall that RSD in 2006–2007 tested students in mathematics and reading, but only through tenth grade. That means the Jefferson students who were in tenth grade at the time of the closure entered new schools in eleventh grade. These students did not take statewide tests during the transition year, so it was not possible to track their post-closure test score trends. However, ninth graders in the closure year were in tenth grade during the transition year. Their achieve-ment—which had already seen a dramatic post-closure decline in 2006—continued to slide in 2007. Test scores for the typical displaced student (an FRPL-eligible racial minority) dropped another 3 points in math and 16 in reading.

Two comparison groups will help put these declines in context. First, historic score trends at Jefferson may provide the best avail-able prediction of what would have occurred had the school not been closed. Two test administrations post-closure, the score gap between displaced students and historic Jefferson students (fitting the same demographic profile) stood at 46 points in math and 70 points in reading. That is 2.3 years of typical score growth in math and 3.7 years in reading.[10]

Of course, there may have been districtwide trends in 2006 and 2007 that make historical comparisons inappropriate. In that event, it would make more sense to compare displaced students to their grade-level peers across RSD. These contemporary comparisons, however, did not yield any better news. Two test administrations post-closure, the score gap between displaced students and other RSD students (again fitting the same demographic profile) stood at 64 points in math and 69 points in reading. That is 4.6 years of typi-cal score growth in math and 6.5 years in reading.[11] Score trends over time for displaced students, historic Jefferson students, and other RSD students are illustrated in figure 4.1.[12]

These effects—especially the reading gap—are almost unbeliev-ably large. It is reasonable to suspect some of each gap is attribut-able to students feeling less motivated to give their best effort on the standardized tests that fed RSD's accountability system. For that rea-son we will later examine outcomes in which the students themselves had a higher stake (for example, graduation). For now, it is worth noting the significance of two consecutive years of decreasing scores. Other researchers have found, as we did, that closures prompt an ini-tial drop in test scores. However, those studies showed that test scores

FIGURE 4.1 Test scores over time for minority, FRPL-eligible students, by test subject

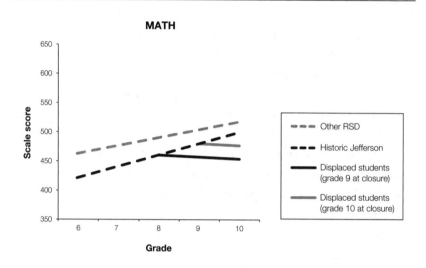

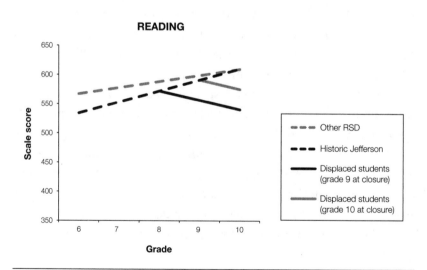

rebounded—or at least stopped declining—in subsequent years.[13] We found no evidence of such a test score turnaround in 2007.

Academics: Student Voices

Not surprisingly, about half of the displaced students who took part in the qualitative study thought the classes in their new schools were harder than classes at Jefferson. One-third reported the academics were equivalent, and one-eighth reported their new classes were easier. Of course, "harder" classes are not necessarily a bad thing. To the extent that harder coursework means more challenging material and higher academic standards, the transition to new schools would represent a beneficial change. Some students did note their new schools offered more rigorous academics. One student, reflecting on the opportunity to write multiple ten-page papers, said, "I never done one before."

More commonly, however, students thought their new schools were harder because they missed the individualized attention available at Jefferson. Displaced students found their relationships with teachers were weaker at the new schools, and according to survey, interview, and focus group data, fewer close relationships meant less academic support. Survey respondents said that "teachers don't explain the work that we have to do" and noted that "at Jefferson . . . if you didn't understand something, you got help right away."

Other students felt somewhat intimidated and frustrated by their new classroom environments. One student elaborated on these struggles at his new school, just before he dropped out: "You try to ask for help and they look at you like you're stupid because you're falling behind . . . [The teacher's] like, 'you have to talk to me after class and make an appointment for another day' . . . Back in Jefferson . . . you just come to class and tell the teacher to help you."

Thanks in part to its dwindling student population, class sizes at Jefferson were typically smaller than in the new schools. Jefferson students' academic struggles prior to the closure were well documented and few would argue the school was on a promising path; nonetheless, displaced students felt comfortable seeking guidance and support from the teachers with whom they had formed close bonds. The closure cut those ties, and displaced students seemed to flounder academically in the transition year. Although survey respondents did acknowledge their new schools offered "more opportunities" and "more programs," disrupted relationships made it difficult for displaced students to translate academic opportunity to academic success.

Thus far, stories and statistics from the transition year are decidedly gloomy. Few students reflected positively on their classroom interactions, and displaced students' test score gaps had grown astonishingly large. Still, absent any other corroborating data these patterns could be explained away. Of course students felt their new classes were harder—higher expectations and increased academic rigor were exactly what these displaced students needed. Of course their test scores dipped for a couple of years—how could we expect displaced students to give their best effort on the very tests that had forced their high school's closure? A rescue mission is about ends, not means. If the closure helped Jefferson students stay in school and ultimately earn a diploma, this policy's benefits might outweigh its costs.

Dropout and Graduation

Analyzing the closure's impact on dropout and graduation required many years of data. The district provided us with "exit records" for Jefferson students (some of whom later became displaced students) for the academic years 2002–2003 through 2006–2007. Exit records essentially tell us the reason for a student's exit from RSD; sometimes the reason for an exit is dropout, and other times it is graduation. Multiple years of exit records allowed us to establish patterns of dropout and graduation, which may (or may not) have changed following the Jefferson closure in 2006.

DROPOUT For the dropout analysis, we defined the "post-closure" years as 2005–2006 and 2006–2007. We included 2005–2006 in the post-closure period because some students in the qualitative study indicated dropping out in spring 2006 in response to the closure announcement. It therefore seemed reasonable to suspect that the closure announcement itself—not just the transition to new schools—prompted some students to exit early. As with the analysis of test score trends, we controlled for student demographics (FRPL, English language learner status, special education status, and race).[14] We also controlled for academic achievement, which is a powerful predictor of dropping out. To hold academic achievement constant in this presentation, we will discuss dropout rates for the "average achiever"—students whose standardized test scores were close to the mean.[15] We also contextualize our findings by describing trends for the typical Jefferson student: an FRPL-eligible racial minority.

Analyses of dropout rates over time revealed a troubling trend, though perhaps not surprising given the qualitative and quantitative findings we have presented thus far. Prior to the closure announcement, the average achiever's probability of dropping out was 7 percent. After the closure announcement and during the transition year, that probability jumped to 15 percent. That is a 114 percent increase. The Jefferson closure announcement was clearly followed by a significant increase in students' odds of an early exit, but there are a couple of caveats worth noting. First, dropout rates had been increasing each year prior to the closure, so we cannot definitively say that the announcement itself caused the increases we report here. In addition, if we were to define the post-closure year as only 2006–2007, the typical displaced student's dropout probability increased from 8 percent to 16 percent—a mere 100 percent increase. Given these ambiguities in the dropout findings, it is especially important to take a close look at trends in graduation.

GRADUATION For the graduation analysis, we consider 2006–2007 the post-closure year. It seemed unreasonable to think a Jefferson student would fail to graduate simply because the closure was announced in the spring of his or her senior year. The graduation rate is simply the percentage of twelfth graders who graduate in a given year, controlling for the same demographic and achievement variables we introduced in the dropout section (FRPL, English language learner status, special education status, and race). Again, we present graduation rate trends for average achievers fitting the demographic profile of the typical Jefferson student, and again the news is not good.

Prior to the closure, an FRPL-eligible minority at Jefferson with average academic achievement had a 71 percent chance of earning a diploma. After the closure, that student's graduation probability dropped to 49 percent—a 31 percent decrease. The caveats to the dropout analysis do not apply here. Graduation rates at Jefferson had not been declining prior to the closure. In fact, they had held steady for each year prior to 2006–2007.

If test score trends could be dismissed as student dissatisfaction, dropout trends as dependent on analytic choices, and qualitative results as highly subjective (we believe none of these can be fully dismissed as such), the graduation rate trends are probably the evidentiary nail in the coffin. The closure looks like a policy that backfired.

Before we move on to our final set of qualitative findings, we should acknowledge that although they are the focus of our analysis, displaced students were not the only intended beneficiaries of the Jefferson closure. The school reopened in 2007–2008 to a new cohort of ninth graders and the promise of a transformation. Jefferson expanded by one grade in each subsequent year until the first "new" students graduated in 2011. Although in its initial years the reopened Jefferson high school showed some promising student achievement gains, progress quickly stalled. Now the school once again posts the lowest test scores in RSD, and its principal was asked to leave in early 2014.

Responding to Adversity

Not all the news in the post-closure years was unequivocally negative. We also asked students to reflect on their transition experiences, specifically asking if they felt they were being successful at their new schools. A surprisingly high number—62 percent—responded in the affirmative. It seemed that in their new school environments, many displaced students had adopted a pragmatic approach to finishing their K–12 careers. They focused on completing the steps required to graduate. As one student noted, "I don't have feelings for this school because I only came here to be able to graduate." Another echoed this sentiment: "Some students . . . weren't going to try to make new friends . . . they were just going to . . . get through it and go on about their business."

We call this response to adversity "adopting a resilient stance." Some displaced students just tried to make the best of a disruptive and difficult transition. They focused on earning a diploma and completing the steps required to move on to postsecondary endeavors. Narrowing their goals and adopting a dispassionate, instrumental view of their remaining high school days allowed them to focus on some important outcomes they could actually control. For some displaced students, the fact that they had managed the closure and the transition and remained in school was, in and of itself, a measure of success.

ASSESSING SCHOOL CLOSURE

Jefferson students and the Jefferson community were angered by the closure. In the transition year, students expressed frustration—even exasperation—with trying to fit in at new schools and succeed academically. Though some adopted a resilient stance in response to this adversity, our analyses of academic outcomes suggest that for the majority of displaced students, the closure was not beneficial. By most accounts it backfired, making a bad situation worse. Is this the inevitable consequence of our harshest accountability sanctions? To cut to the quick, should we never close schools?

There are, in our estimation, four justifications policy makers might use to close a school: (1) dwindling enrollment has made it financially infeasible to keep the school open; (2) "rebooting" the school for new cohorts of students might make it easier for leaders to establish a culture conducive to learning; (3) closing schools improves public education by sending a firm message that inadequate academic progress will not be tolerated; and (4) the students displaced by the closure will be better off in new schools.[16] Of course, these justifications are not mutually exclusive. One can make a case that all four were argued in support of the Jefferson closure.

Our empirical analyses focus on the fourth reason (displaced students will benefit), so our central recommendations will focus on some ways school districts can avoid repeating RSD's mistakes. But let us first evaluate the other reasons to close a school, starting with the most intuitive: diminishing enrollment. When a school district is financially strapped, maintaining a building serving few students does not make much sense. The expenditure required to keep nearly empty buildings operational could be put to better use in other schools, benefitting both students and financial stability districtwide. Whether displaced students will benefit is an open question (one we believe our analyses inform), but the answer may be immaterial to the closure decision itself. Closing schools to stave off insolvency is not about incentivizing academic improvement or reinventing a school's culture. It is about fiscal sustainability, and in some districts that might take precedence.

The next two reasons—closing a school and later reopening it to transform its culture, or closing schools to generally incentivize educational improvement—rely on more tenuous assumptions. For the first, we must assume that (1) there are skilled and seasoned professionals available to staff the reopened school, (2) those professionals can instill a school culture meaningfully different from the one that preceded it even if struggles associated with poverty in the surrounding neighborhood remain the same, and (3) the transformation in culture will lead to improved academic outcomes. Our research in RSD did not focus on the rebirth of Jefferson, but the reopened school's struggles subsequent to 2008 suggest transformation is just as hard as it sounds.

If the "transformation" logic model is far-fetched, the "closure as educational motivator" rationale seems positively outlandish. To believe closures would effectively make an example of underperforming schools and discourage failure elsewhere, we must assume that educators believe (1) closed schools' contexts reflect their own contexts, (2) schools are closed because educators have failed to deliver academic improvement, and (3) through instructional improvements they can succeed where others have failed and to the degree required to avoid closure. We are unaware of any research studies that have empirically tested this specific chain of reasoning. But there are quite a few studies that point to minimal positive effects associated with accountability sanctions under No Child Left Behind.[17] We do not mean to dismiss the notion of accountability altogether. We simply mean to examine its most severe manifestation—school closure—and ask whether such a sanction is ever prudent, given the collateral damage it has been shown to inflict.

The last reason to close schools is to improve educational outcomes for displaced students. On this point, there is empirical evidence. Ours is admittedly a case study and we are not the only researchers to have examined the topic. Other studies have focused on school closures in Illinois, Michigan, and Ohio, and from those analyses some common themes emerge. First, displaced students can expect to see measures of academic achievement (test scores) decline immediately following the closure. However, these studies find that after two to three years of transition, test scores can be expected to level off if not begin rising again.[18] By contrast, while we did observe steep declines in test scores immediately following the Jefferson closure, we did not see those declines end during the transition year. Each study (ours included) emphasizes that post-closure outcomes will depend heavily on the availability of other high performing district schools to which displaced students can transfer.

Since the research on long-term closure effects is mixed, it is probably safest to say that displaced students will not necessarily be better off in new schools. Therefore it would seem school closure is generally inadvisable without a powerful rationale. The demonstrated costs seem too high given the limited proven benefits. Closing a school may help a district avoid financial catastrophe—and that is a legitimate reason to do it—but districts should avoid predictions that closures on their own will beget academic turnarounds. Most evidence points to the contrary.

AVOIDING BACKFIRE IN SCHOOL CLOSURE

All this said, we take a pragmatic position and acknowledge it is likely that for the foreseeable future schools will continue to close for the reasons we have outlined.[19] How, then, can districts make the best of a difficult situation for affected communities and students and avoid policy backfire?

The answer to this question should start with an examination of what led Jefferson students to endure such a difficult post-closure experience, especially when other closure studies have documented test score turnarounds for displaced students, at least after a while. For such "how" and "why" questions, qualitative data are particularly useful—indispensable, we argue, for drawing implications from closure research. Our qualitative data point to three features of displaced students' experiences that were central to the Jefferson case, and these features may suggest some constructive recommendations. First, Jefferson students and the broader community did not have the opportunity to participate in the closure decision-making process. Second, unlike other closures explored in the research literature, which almost always focuses on elementary and middle school students, this one affected high school students.[20] Teenagers are navigating a critical period of psychosocial development, and closures may sever tight bonds between students, their school peers, and trusted adults. High schoolers have more autonomy and may see dropping out as a reasonable response. Third, other studies have underscored the importance of high-quality in-district alternatives for displaced students. When schools close, affected students need demonstrably better options, and our data suggest few such options existed for the Jefferson cohort.

These distinctions—high school students in a segregated district facing a forced diaspora—make the Jefferson story different from most of the peer-reviewed research, but not unique. By way of summarizing lessons learned in RSD and prodding further research, we conclude this chapter with four recommendations for districts contemplating school closure:

- **Involve affected students and communities in a robust, democratic decision-making process.** Arguments against school closure are about more than test scores; they are driven by a normative claim that families and students have a right to participate in decisions that affect their schools and communities. This is a right that is too often disregarded in decisions about schools serving communities of color. When school systems undertake community engagement efforts, they are often focused more on marketing a particular decision than deliberating about it. More substantive and open democratic processes require time and attention to differences of power and privilege.[21] In addition to the normative rationale for robust participation, if students and families play a legitimate role in policy decisions, and ultimately decide that closure is an acceptable option, those affected are more likely to understand the reasons behind the decision, take ownership of the transition, and get invested in the outcomes. Multiple studies have shown that getting students involved in public decision making is developmentally appropriate for high-school-age youth.[22]
- **Ensure that there are enough higher performing district schools with adequate capacity to receive and educate displaced students.** This step should seem intuitive, but research has shown that some displaced students struggle to find new

schools that have both a tradition of strong academic performance and the capacity (for example, manageable class sizes)
to accept and integrate those who transfer from closed schools.
Often the "best" schools are also overenrolled already. Information about the receiving schools' academic performance
and programmatic emphases should be made available far in
advance of the closure, so displaced students and their families
can make informed decisions about new schools. If there are
no district schools with adequate capacity to enroll displaced
students or academic programs that suit their needs, a district
should reconsider the wisdom of closing a school.

- **Keep track of displaced students after the closure, and pro-
actively connect them with mentors at their new schools.** No
matter the reason for school closure, districts should take responsibility for maximizing displaced students' chances for
success. This means, at the outset, documenting which students transfer to which schools, and later tracking their progress in those schools, including achievement test scores,
grades, persistence (that is, staying in school and advancing
in grade level), and graduation. Positive outcomes on all these
metrics will depend on displaced students successfully inte-
grating in their new schools. Therefore, districts should also
pair every displaced student with a mentor at his or her new
school to facilitate a sense of belonging. Mentors will not completely solve the problem (see the preceding point), but they
can at least help connect students with robust academic support services to ease the post-closure transition. Additional
work can be done in the receiving schools to prepare teachers
and administrative staff for the incoming students, including
ways to address the stigma those displaced students may face.

- **Articulate and empirically test the school closure theory of
action.** Closure is a form of forced student mobility, and mobility tends to depress academic performance, especially when

it is externally imposed.[23] If closures are to continue, it is imperative that districts articulate the reasons for a closure and its intended outcomes, and subsequently test whether those outcomes were realized. On this point, educational agencies should not defer to academics to do the research. School closure decisions will impose hardships on displaced students; it is foolish to pretend otherwise. It is therefore incumbent on the decision makers to show that these disruptive policy choices confer benefits that outweigh their inevitable costs.

FIVE

When School Choice Policies Backfire

Why New Options for Parents Can Become New Barriers to Equity

Carolyn Sattin-Bajaj

The unprecedented expansion of school choice policies in districts across the United States and internationally in the past two decades has had a dramatic impact on the educational experiences of and options available to students today. With charter school laws enacted in forty-two states and the District of Columbia and some form of school choice (including magnet schools, voucher programs, and inter- or intradistrict enrollment) operating in a total of forty-six states, the choice of where a child attends *public* school has now become the norm rather than the exception.[1] School choice is no longer reserved for the wealthy few who can afford private school tuition or those who have the financial freedom to choose where to live based on the quality of the public schools.

New York City features prominently among the large urban, and, increasingly, the ex- and suburban districts that have embraced school choice as a driver of education reform and improvement. In fact, the idea of a "portfolio model" of schooling in which the district administration functions as the high-level manager of a broad array of educational options (including charter schools, district public schools, and a combination of virtual, hybrid, and nontraditional school models) has become one of the latest educational "innovations" being championed by education leaders, funders, and policy makers—although it is not without detractors.[2] In New York City parents may participate in choice at every stage of their child's public education—from prekindergarten onward—through open enrollment policies, magnet programs, controlled choice plans, and charter schools. The district's extensive investment in school choice policies is evidenced by the rapid growth of the charter sector and an ever-expanding number of choice options at the preK, primary, and secondary school levels. According to the most recent data published by the New York Charter Center, as of October 2014 there were 197 charter schools serving approximately 83,000 students in New York City, or roughly 6 percent of the public school population.[3] It is the long-standing mandatory high school choice policy, however, that continues to be the New York City Department of Education's (NYC-DOE) crowning jewel. It is widely touted by school officials as a policy lever that can provide families with abundant choice options while simultaneously increasing equity across the district.

Some version of high school choice has existed in New York City since the 1960s. Today, under the current mandatory high school choice policy, all eighth-grade students who wish to attend a district public high school must submit a single application form ranking up to twelve high school programs out of seven hundred possibilities citywide (this is separate from the charter school lotteries that operate outside of the high school choice process). The official goals for the high school choice policy, which was revised in 2004, are to increase both choice and equity for New York City public school families. One direct intention of this policy was to expand the educational access and opportunities of low-income students, who have historically attended the worst schools in the poorest neighborhoods, by allowing them to apply to attend any school across the city. To that end, the current high school "matching" formula was designed to improve the likelihood that a student would be assigned to a school that he or she ranked highly on the application and to distribute low achieving students as evenly as possible across high schools.[4] At the same time, however, the choice policy has created additional barriers for students and parents that, in many instances, serve to impede, rather than facilitate, easier access to high-quality school options. These barriers come in the form of districtwide and school-level admissions requirements, policies, and practices ranging from mandating lottery participation for high-demand charter schools and using one high-stakes standardized examination to determine admission to the most elite public "specialized" high schools to requesting or requiring portfolio materials, auditions, and interviews at certain highly sought-after, academically rigorous schools. Even the "limited unscreened schools," smaller schools that do not screen based on students' prior academic performance, give priority admission to those students who attend an open house, tour, or other event. Such requirements have been found to be particularly onerous to the lowest performing and most disadvantaged students, resulting in their being less likely to prepare for exams, auditions, and interviews or to attend open houses or events that confer priority admissions status.[5]

It is not surprising, then, that despite the NYCDOE's intention to use school choice policies as an engine for educational equity, there is little evidence to date that school choice is successfully serving this function. To start, New York City remains one of the most racially segregated school districts in the country; this is in part due to an arduous and confusing set of admissions criteria, which, in turn, contribute to the backfire of school choice policies. For example, in their recent report on school segregation across New York State, Kucsera and Orfield found that 73 percent of charter schools were considered "apartheid schools," or schools in which less than 1 percent of students are White.[6] Charter schools in New York City have also consistently underenrolled some of the hardest and most expensive-to-serve student populations, particularly English language learners.[7] In terms of high school choice specifically, researchers have found that on average, eighth-grade students in New York City are matched to high schools that mirror the socioeconomic and racial/ethnic makeup of their feeder middle schools despite the students ranking more racially and socioeconomically diverse schools higher on their applications.[8]

Just as significant, evidence shows that rather than expanding options, school choice policies have, at best, maintained constricted access to a limited supply of high performing schools, and, at worst, created additional barriers for the most disadvantaged students' access to the highest-quality options.[9] Students of color, who also constitute the majority of New York City's low-income population, are disproportionately enrolled in low performing schools across the city and are underrepresented in the most elite and desirable schools and programs at the primary and secondary levels.[10] A recent report released by the New York City Independent Budget Office showed that of all of the students enrolled in the city's most selective "specialized" high schools, only 11 percent came from the lowest-income census tracts, compared to 26 percent of students coming from the top income quintile in the 2012–2013 school year.[11] This income-based disparity is mirrored by racial/ethnic enrollment gaps, with the latest figures showing that only 12 percent of students offered placement in the specialized high schools during the 2014–2015 admissions cycle were Black or Latino, even though they make up roughly 70 percent of the total student population.[12] The latest results are consistent with recent admissions patterns that have triggered a civil rights complaint charging that the specialized high school admissions policy is racially discriminatory. This complaint, filed by the NAACP and other civil rights groups, is currently under review at the US Department of Education.[13]

The flip side of the uneven distribution of students across the district's most desirable schools is the fact that the city's most marginalized students are overrepresented in the elementary, middle, and high schools that have demonstrated the weakest capacity to prepare students for academic success, including competitive high school admissions and college-level work.[14] It is not possible to empirically examine the counterfactual for all students—that is, to compare students' actual high school assignments to the performance metrics and demographic composition of the high schools to which they would have been assigned if the choice policy were not in place—because many of the former zoned high schools have been closed. In other words, a large proportion of students are left without a default zoned school. However, some research has shown that in many cases students' assigned high schools are scarcely better—and sometimes worse—than the sending neighborhood middle schools and/or high schools that they would have attended in the absence of a compulsory choice policy.[15]

In theory, eliminating residential zoning requirements for school enrollment and making all high schools available to students from across New York City's five boroughs sounds like a promising strategy to attack long-standing patterns of disparate distribution of educational opportunities and outcomes by students' racial/ethnic and socioeconomic background. Yet the promise of choice is not being realized; rather, on many accounts, it appears to be backfiring as a consequence of new barriers that put higher-quality options virtually out of reach for many of the most disadvantaged students in the system. This chapter draws on data collected through a case study of a New York City middle school implementing the choice policy during two academic years (2008–2009 and 2009–2010) to describe some of the possible reasons for this policy's tepid response to long-standing segregation and unequal distribution of educational access and ultimate backfire. The backfire of the high school choice policy explored in this chapter cannot be understood as a phenomenon in isolation; rather, it is the culmination of a series of backfires of school choice policies at every level of schooling (preK through high school) that have thwarted school integration and consistently blocked the neediest students from accessing the best schools in the city. This has happened through the creation of competitive choice processes playing out on an unequal field in which students with more resources gain entry to the most desirable schools early on (e.g., being admitted to gifted and talented programs in elementary school, or accessing high performing middle schools through the middle school choice policy), thereby virtually ensuring an interrupted journey from elite elementary school to elite high school. In fact, the backfire of the high school choice policy might be better understood as just one symptom of the backfire of a broader portfolio strategy that relies too heavily on free-market-based theories of choice unleashed without intervention.

In essence, the high school choice policy failed to deliver on its promise via three fundamental errors. First, the policy was based on assumptions about parental involvement and access to resources that were out of sync with actual behaviors and practices of predominantly low-income, minority students and families. The district took for granted a significant amount of parental input and investment in school search and decision making. Therefore, students with parents who already had sufficient access to resources and time jumped ahead of the curve in choosing a high school, while those whose parents did not fell dramatically behind in terms of making strategic and informed school selections.[16] Next, the policy was designed with unrealistic expectations of intensive student engagement in school search activities. As with parents, those students who already had high engagement tended to be White, of higher socioeconomic status, or of higher academic ability. Thus, we see these highly engaged students better positioned to identify and gain admission to higher performing schools, and those with less engagement being relegated—as a result of their own uninformed choice or district assignment—to lower performing schools. Last, the district failed to require that middle schools provide even the most basic information and guidance to students and parents about how to engage in a thoughtful school choice process. This chapter will focus on the final issue—the failure to require and oversee school-based efforts to inform families about high school choice—and describe the significance of the glaring absence of accountability for school choice in a context dominated by educational accountability in other arenas. The chapter will explore some of the possible causes and consequences of the lack of established mandates about school personnel's responsibilities to students and parents vis-à-vis high school choice and show evidence from a case-study middle school of the impact of low-income, immigrant-origin students and families receiving minimal assistance with their high school applications.

A LOOK INSIDE HIGH SCHOOL CHOICE IN NEW YORK CITY

Each year an estimated eighty thousand eighth-grade students participate in high school choice in New York City. In the fall of their eighth-grade year students receive an application form and are asked to choose twelve options from among seven hundred programs in approximately four hundred public high schools citywide. These programs vary widely in size, theme/academic focus, eligibility requirements, selection method, extracurricular activities, and academic outcomes, among other characteristics. Despite the large number of schools and programs in New York City, there continues to be a shortage of high performing high schools even after decades of reform. According to an analysis from the Center for New York City Affairs at the New School, only 38.3 percent of schools with graduating classes in 2007 had graduation rates of 75 percent or higher.[17] Analysis of more recent data released by the New York City Department of Education found that by 2011, the percentage of high schools with graduation rates of 75 percent or above had declined slightly to 34 percent (143 out of a total of 421 high schools); this figure drops to 20.2 percent of high schools (or a total of 85) when the new Regents diploma requirements are used.[18] Thus, high school assignments stand to have significant impact on students' educational chances.

District leadership is keenly aware of the current undersupply of high-quality educational options for students across the city and frequently makes comments to this effect at public events. In response, the NYCDOE has relied heavily on school accountability measures to identify high and low performing schools and has avidly pursued closure or reconstitution of persistently underperforming schools, although less so under the current administration of Chancellor Carmen Fariña, whose approach to school reform represents a marked departure from that of her recent predecessor, Joel Klein.[19] NYCDOE officials have consistently pointed to the power of parent demand in a school choice marketplace to weed out the underperforming schools and reward the successful ones with high popularity, echoing the arguments of school choice proponents for decades; however, the supply and demand issue persists, and the least advantaged, predominantly minority students continue to be funneled to the worst schools at higher rates than their higher-income peers.[20]

One study of the high school choices and placements of New York City students scoring in the bottom 20 percent on seventh-grade math and English tests from 2007 to 2011 found that low achieving students chose—and were therefore assigned to—lower performing high schools (as measured by attendance and graduation rates) than their higher performing peers.[21] In another study that considered a broader set of student background factors, Corcoran and Levin found variation by poverty status, race/ethnicity, gender, and special education and English language learner (ELL) classification in the number of high schools New York City students applied to and in the quality of high school assignments (as measured by graduation rates, admissions standards, and school suspension rates).[22] Finally, Meade and colleagues found that Black and Latino students in New York City were concentrated in high schools that received the worst Progress Report grades from the city (A–F ratings).[23] These results point to a complicated set of interconnected policies and practices that hinder progress toward greater educational equity through mechanisms such as choice; the lack of coherence between New York City's accountability policies and school choice policies lies at the heart of the problem.

EDUCATION AND ACCOUNTABILITY

The role of accountability systems in contributing to, rather than counteracting, the trends in race- and income-based determinants of educational opportunity has become a lightning rod in the ongoing debates about inequities in students' access to high-quality schooling. Accountability systems that use student performance on high-stakes tests and other evaluations to assess districts, schools, principals, teachers, and students are a defining feature of the educational land-scape in the United States today, codified in state and federal education legislation. As a result of these accountability regimes, schools operate under tremendous pressure to meet performance targets or risk severe sanctions. At the same time, many school districts like New York City are pursuing purportedly equity-driven reforms such as school choice alongside accountability. However, the implementation and outcomes of some of these policies are neither monitored to the same extent as student performance nor measured or tied to rewards and punishments. The inconsistency with which districts invest in and evaluate different policies raises questions about what is being communicated to school-level administrators, faculty, and staff about district priorities, how they respond to these signals, and what their responses mean for the success of the policies and their impact on students.

New York City provides an illustrative case of the complexity of balancing choice, accountability, equity, and access in the twenty-first-century education landscape. New York City's accountability system, launched during the 2007–2008 school year, was designed to "hold schools accountable for student achievement and provide[s] data, tools, and resources that educators and families [could] use to improve schools and support student learning."[24] It was built in parallel to the state accountability system and was developed as a tool to track schools' progress toward the requirement that all students meet minimum state proficiency levels in English language arts, mathematics, and science; to show student growth; and to disaggregate student achievement data by key subgroups. At the time of data collection for the study discussed in this chapter (2008–2010), an annual school Progress Report was the NYCDOE's primary accountability tool, and it combined measures of a school's student proficiency levels with student growth measures, external inspections, and public satisfaction scores (from the Learning Environment Survey). Whereas schools that received Progress Report grades of C, D, or F for multiple years would be subject to leadership change, restructuring, or even closure, schools that earned high grades received financial bonuses that could reach into the tens of thousands of dollars for principals and teachers.[25] The Learning Environment Survey was distributed annually to students, parents, and teachers to measure satisfaction with their schools across a number of domains. The results of the survey—both in terms of reported level of satisfaction and overall response rate—factored directly into each school's annual Progress Report grade.

In the era of testing and accountability, schools that serve the most disadvantaged populations are being called on to provide more intensive supports to help all students reach academic proficiency. These same schools are often under the most intense scrutiny and pressure from the local and state education officials to improve student outcomes on standardized tests. As a result, they logically organize themselves and distribute resources to meet the benchmarks for which they will be rewarded and pay less attention to policies for which they will not be judged. The case study of one low performing middle school's treatment of the mandatory high school choice policy provides an example of this kind of rational response—a response that reveals an unintended consequence of accountability systems that exclude some policies and programs (such as school-level investment in preparing students for high school choice) from school evaluations. The backfire of the high school choice policy in New York City is just one among many of the unintended consequences associated with fervent adoption of the types of accountability policy in place in New York and elsewhere; however, given the predictive power of school quality for students' life-course outcomes, it is an extraordinarily detrimental one.[26]

Research on the wide-ranging impacts of accountability policies has identified a variety of ways in which accountability plans may complicate, and in some cases, thwart efforts to seek equity in education. Studies have found widespread use of "gaming" strategies to meet benchmarks—such as reclassifying low-income and low performing students as requiring special education, and focusing on "bubble kids" who sit at the margins of the desired proficiency levels—and a strong correspondence between school-level demographics and the likelihood of a school's receiving sanctions.[27] This chapter addresses questions about the backfire of one district's school choice policy by examining it within the broader, powerful accountability context in which it operated. A comparison of the school-level implementation of two of the NYCDOE's signature initiatives—the compulsory high school choice policy and the Learning Environment Survey (now called the NYC School Survey), only the latter of which factors into the district's accountability framework—reveals the far-reaching impact of the district's disparate treatment of the policies, in terms of both school personnel's responses to them and students' understanding of and preparedness to negotiate the labyrinthine school choice process. Ultimately, this disparity helps, in part, to explain how the school choice policy is contributing to a retreat from, rather than advancement toward, greater integration and a more equitable distribution of educational opportunity among New York City's immensely diverse, although predominantly low-income and minority, student population.

RESEARCH DESIGN AND METHODOLOGY

The findings presented in this chapter come from data collected through ethnographic observations of school-based activities related to high school choice at a case-study middle school site and interviews conducted with school personnel at the case-study site. The chapter draws from a larger study of eighth-grade students' and families' experiences with high school choice in New York City, which is presented in its entirety in the book *Unaccompanied Minors: Immigrant Youth, School Choice, and the Pursuit of Equity.*[28]

Case-Study Site

A single case-study middle school was selected for this study on the basis of its size, the student population served, and its academic offerings. IS 725 was selected as the focal middle school primarily because it approximated the type of middle schools that low-income Latino youth living in urban areas have been shown to attend in terms of size, student demographic makeup, and academic outcomes.[29] The Harvard Civil Rights Project reports that Black and Latino students are three times as likely as White students to be in high-poverty schools, they attend predominantly minority schools in disproportionate numbers, and they are more likely to be enrolled in schools identified as low performing.[30] IS 725 was large (having approximately twenty-one hundred students in grades six through eight), historically low performing (only 45.2 percent of students scored at proficiency on the New York State mathematics exam in 2008–2009), high poverty (81 percent of students qualified for free lunch in 2009–2010), and had a high concentration of minority students (98.2 percent non-White) and a high proportion of English language learners (37.9 percent). Eighty percent of students enrolled at IS 725 were classified as "Hispanic" in 2009–2010, and these students were primarily first- and second-generation children of Latin American and Caribbean immigrants from the Dominican Republic, Mexico, and Ecuador. Twelve percent of students were classified as

"Asian," followed by 6 percent "Black" and a small number of "White" students. The middle school was divided into five separate "academies," each with a dedicated assistant principal and guidance counselor, and the school's academic offerings included Spanish and Chinese bilingual education classes and a gifted and talented magnet program.

School-Based Ethnographic Observations

Ethnographic observations conducted over the course of two academic years at IS 725 serve as the primary data source for this chapter. Between September 2008 and June 2010, I engaged in over four hundred hours of fieldwork at IS 725, during which time I observed in detail how school personnel implemented the high school choice policy. Specifically, I was interested in understanding who was responsible for overseeing high school choice at the school level, what resources were allocated to informing students and parents about how the process worked, where it fell among the school leadership's priorities, and how school personnel felt about the high school choice process and their roles in it. I spent much of my time shadowing the five guidance counselors while they engaged in choice-related activities such as distributing applications and conducting presentations for groups of students. I also conducted informal interviews with each of the five guidance counselors and observed their interactions with students who sought advice or assistance with the application. Finally, I met with the principal on at least five occasions to learn more about his goals for the school and interacted with other administrators, school support staff, and eighth-grade teachers on a regular basis.

Data Analysis

A combination of deductive and inductive techniques was used to analyze the data. I combined *a priori* themes based on the guiding questions of this research project with grounded theory that emerged directly from the data. Analyzed as a whole, the ethnographic and interview data highlighted the sharp contrast between the low-priority status of high school choice and the highly engaged school-level response to policies linked to the Progress Report grade.

In what follows, I explore this contrast by describing how the school personnel at IS 725 did and did not work to guide and inform students and parents about the high school choice policy. First, I show the middle school administration's negligible interest in high school choice and the progressive decline in information and guidance activities provided to students and parents. Next, I present data from the middle school guidance counselors about their roles, responsibilities, and activities vis à vis the high school choice process, focusing specifically on the (minimal) steps they took to explain the process to students and parents. Last, I compare the tepid school-based outreach about high school choice with school personnel's extensive efforts to improve parent response rate on the Learning Environment Survey. Repeated examples of the school principal's direct engagement in promoting programs and activities that could improve students' standardized test scores provide additional evidence of the degree to which accountability influenced school-level priorities, contributing in part to the backfire of the school choice policy.

HIGH SCHOOL CHOICE AS A LOW-PRIORITY POLICY

In spite of the well-established significance of the transition to high school for adolescent development and achievement and the NYC-DOE's public pronouncements of the centrality of choice in its strategic reform efforts, the high school choice process proved to be an issue of minimal consequence to the school administration and guidance counselors at IS 725.[31] Middle schools in New York City maintain significant autonomy in determining how to work with families on high school choice, and their activities are neither monitored nor measured in any evaluation by the NYCDOE. In the absence of oversight, mandates, incentives, or sanctions, students and families at IS

725 received minimal assistance with their high school applications and were left to negotiate the complex system alone.

The school's failure to host even a single informational event for parents about the high school choice process in the fall, even after having organized a successful workshop for 250 parents the previous year, is perhaps the greatest indication of the policy's low-priority status at IS 725. Guidance counselors offered varied explanations for why no event was held in the second year of the study. For example, one of the counselors, Ms. Perolli, told me, "There isn't going to be a workshop this year. I don't know what happened. Ms. Torres [the community coordinator] is in charge of organizing it. Maybe because she's pregnant, she wasn't feeling that great at the beginning of the year. I'm not going to say anything." Others cited budget cuts and new performance pressures on the principal. Regardless of the reason, there was no demonstrated concern on the part of school counselors or school administrators that no event had been planned, nor was there evidence of any monitoring of what and how information about high school choice was conveyed to eighth-grade students and parents at IS 725. Rather, the lack of event went unnoticed—one of many examples of the negligible attention that high school choice received more generally.

Guidance Counselors' Approaches to Informing Students About High School Choice

With caseloads of approximately four hundred students across grades six through eight, on any given day a guidance counselor at IS 725 might be leading a mandated counseling session, participating in a disciplinary meeting, conducting an exit interview for a student who has been discharged, and/or processing a new student enrollment. High school choice was yet another task to tackle in the teeming pile of bureaucratic responsibilities.

Taking cues from the school leadership, guidance counselors at IS 725 ultimately treated the high school choice process as a necessary chore, and they attempted to minimize its demands on their time. They did so even while knowing that many of their eighth-grade students were unprepared to make informed school selections. In fact, guidance counselors actually expected that many students and parents would be confused about the choice process and anticipated that they would be unhappy with their final high school assignments. One of the bilingual school counselors, Mr. Sanchez, relayed this expectation to me, saying, "It's a lot of information. Parents don't understand it. I can never cover it in one period. The kids don't get it, but the parents are worse." Yet, rather than increase outreach efforts or change their approaches to working with students on high school choice, the counselors relied on the same communication strategies year after year to explain the process—even when they had thoughts about how those efforts could be improved or increased.

It was not the case that the guidance counselors did not understand what might be done to better inform families. On the contrary: over the course of the two years I spent at IS 725, the school counselors clearly articulated ideas and proposals about how to make choice-related information more accessible to them. For instance, as early as the second week of September, when middle schools tend to be in the planning stages of school-based choice events, Ms. Perolli explained, "We should have two Saturdays in October when school is open and we, guidance counselors, are available to answer questions for students and parents." Other school counselors offered similar ideas, including providing simultaneous Spanish translation and augmenting parent-teacher conferences to include individual discussion about high school choices. However, there was neither initiative nor support from the administration to implement new strategies, so the counselors proceeded with what they had done in the past despite being keenly aware of the lackluster outcomes their communication methods produced.

FOCUS ON APPEALS AND APPLICATION DEADLINE In an effort to curtail the time demands of the high school choice process, guidance counselors at IS 725 directed their energies toward collecting a completed application from every eighth-grade student by the deadline and limiting the number of future appeals requests. This narrow focus on meeting a deadline took precedence over counseling students and working with them to identify appropriate schools; "guidance" related to school choice was thus reduced to whole-class instruction about how to correctly fill out the application, grade-level assemblies to explain the contents of the High School Directory, and targeted reminders about returning the application by the deadline. Virtually no personalized advice was provided to the hundreds of low-income and immigrant-origin eighth graders at the school—students who would likely have benefited from additional assistance in making high school choices.

Although school-based activities to assist students with the high school choice process were not evaluated in any of the accountability frameworks, the number of students who appealed their high school assignments and the number of late applications were recorded and could be seen by the principal and administrators at NYCDOE headquarters. Fewer requests for appeals after high schools were assigned also translated into less work on high school applications for guidance counselors and fewer hours spent responding to parents' and students' complaints. Moreover, the NYCDOE has used the number of appeals to gauge public satisfaction with the choice process and has emphasized a decline in this figure in recent years as an indication of its steady improvement.[32]

According to guidance counselors at IS 725, in previous years the majority of appeals were petitioned on the basis of a travel hardship. Therefore, in what appeared to be a strategic move to reduce the probability of future requests for appeals, guidance counselors emphasized school location as an essential criterion for students to consider when evaluating a school. In fact, nearly every time guidance counselors spoke to students about the high school application, either individually or in groups, they mentioned the importance of considering school location and visiting websites to get estimated travel times. The guidance counselors made no effort to hide their desire to limit the number of appeals; in fact, they explicitly stated their justification for repeatedly emphasizing location. Ms. Perolli explained: "Every year they put a school down and they don't go travel to see how far it is. And then when they get it, they decide it is too far . . . I tell them, 'if you put it on there [the application] that means you want to go.' I put it everywhere that they should watch travel time, call the school, take a Saturday [to make the trip]. Then the parents come in [to request an appeal]."

In contrast to their recurrent commentary about the importance of school location, the guidance counselors at IS 725 rarely discussed school performance as a factor to consider in school selection. The guidance counselors' lack of reference to traditional measures of school quality (such as graduation rates, Regents exam passing rates, and college acceptances) or even to newer metrics (like the Progress Report grade) was particularly notable in light of the NYCDOE's substantial investment in creating publicly available accountability reports. Yet, without incentives for ensuring that their eighth-grade students applied to the highest performing schools to which they were eligible—or, conversely, penalties for providing inadequate information to those students—the middle school guidance counselors made a rational decision to highlight the aspect of the application process that had taken much of their time in years past: requests for appeals of high school assignments based on location.

ACCOUNTABILITY DRIVES PRIORITIES

There was a strong correlation between the attention a policy received at IS 725 and the weight it was given in formal school evaluations such as the Progress Report. Examination of school-level allocation of resources, and of the energy and creativity that school staff invested in carrying out tasks related to a particular policy, reveals the way in which the IS 725 administration ordered its priorities. For example, whereas guidance counselors were singularly responsible for all aspects of work related to high school choice, nearly every member of the school community was engaged in efforts to improve parental response rates on the Learning Environment Survey. Both survey outcomes and response rates factored into the school's Progress Report grade, and the resources spent to increase parental response rates far exceeded those allocated to engage parents in the high school choice process. Moreover, the school administration changed its outreach strategy in an attempt to better reach families and encourage more responses on the Learning Environment Survey, while activities related to high school choice were cut back.

Over the course of the same two-year period in which high school choice communication efforts declined, the principal at IS 725 responded to the poor parental response rate on the Learning Environment Survey in the first year (16 percent) by overhauling the outreach strategy and enlisting all five assistant principals in the task of enforcing it. Even though surveys would not be distributed until late February, as early as November the principal, Mr. Polo, began working on plans to change how the school distributed and collected surveys, ultimately requiring homeroom teachers to distribute and collect parent surveys and making the assistant principals responsible for monitoring progress. In addition, he instituted a series of incentives to encourage students to return their parents' surveys, including a schoolwide pizza party given to the academy whose students turned in the highest number of completed parent surveys. Through his direct involvement and the resources he attached to this initiative, Mr. Polo clearly signaled to staff the importance of increasing parent response rate on the Learning Environment Survey.

The pervasive influence of accountability on school priorities was also evident in the messages that the school principal delivered to parents at school-sponsored events. He used every possible occasion—ranging from Back to School night to parent-teacher conferences—to emphasize the importance of preparing students for state assessments and to advertise available academic supports. Given its status at the time of the study as a "School in Need of Improvement" (SINI) by the New York State Education Department (NYSED), IS 725 was under even more intense pressure to raise student test scores on the state mathematics and English language arts examinations or face consequences, including closure. As a result, the principal, assistant principals, and teachers expended tremendous energy publicizing the Supplementary Educational Services (SES) program (a program that provided free tutoring services to low-income students through federal grant monies) and encouraging eligible families to enroll in it. During the first three months of the school year, school staff worked tirelessly to distribute SES information packets to eligible students, host information sessions for parents, organize school-based fairs for SES providers, help parents with registration forms, and repeatedly call and remind families who had enrolled students in SES in previous years to register again. Even at the high school choice workshop held for parents of eighth graders in October 2008, the principal seized the opportunity to remind parents about testing and enrolling in SES: "Now, in order to graduate from eighth grade, students need a minimum of level two in reading and math . . . If you see a 65 or 70 [on their first report card], there is a chance that your child won't pass, and we'll need to get him help now . . . If you didn't fill out forms for SES, you should."

Conversely, the choice process was treated like an afterthought, and something far removed from the core activities of the school. The principal never once made a public statement about high school choice, nor did he use events for seventh- and eighth-grade parents to share information about the choice process.

AVOIDING BACKFIRE IN SCHOOL CHOICE POLICIES

This chapter showed how distortive effects of the accountability system in New York City reached as far as the high school choice policy.

By muddling school personnel's sense of what is most important for students' long-term educational success and diverting attention from what students actually needed from schools in order to make sense of the complex choice system and potentially benefit from the policy—accurate, comprehensible information and clear-cut advice about how to identify appropriate options—the accountability policies did more than just impede the potential for choice to increase disadvantaged students' access to good schools. In reality, the perverse incentive structure established and enforced by the district's accountability framework contributed to the actual backfire of the high school choice policy. This backfire is evidenced by the ongoing and worsening school segregation across New York City and permanent disparities in educational access, opportunity, and outcomes across racial/ethnic and income lines. Year after year, the most marginalized students are in large part unable to gain access to high-quality schooling in New York City's vast, highly unregulated choice marketplace. Yet the district remains steadfast in its belief in the value of giving parents the freedom to choose and in the power of choice to correct historic disequilibria. This belief blinds leaders from seeing what is happening in schools and in students' lives and taking steps to rectify or reverse the backfire. The fact that the choice process plays out as district officials intended for many higher-income students in more advantaged schools—with highly involved parents, more extensive information provided by schools, and more knowledge-based decision making by families—serves only to reinforce district leadership's commitment to the choice policy and its equity potential despite indisputable evidence to the contrary.[33] The troubling irony of students with the most home-based resources also benefitting from richer school-based supports for choice has yet to spur corrective action from NYCDOE officials.

In the end, students and parents at IS 725 were left to navigate the vast universe of high school options with minimal school-based support. None of the necessary foundations were put in place for schools to adequately inform, counsel, and assist students and families with choice, particularly those families who require the most guidance.[34] Without clearly articulated expectations of middle school activities, formal mechanisms for monitoring performance, or adequate provision of resources to defray the associated costs of providing these support services, the choice policy got pushed aside by school personnel who were struggling to manage an endless stream of pressures and demands.

Despite compelling evidence of substantial challenges with current school choice policies and practices, there may be feasible solutions to help stop and potentially even counteract the backfire. Improved information and communication efforts at the district level, coupled with greater resource allocations made specifically to middle schools serving the neediest student populations and earmarked for high school choice guidance, is a start. But such efforts would likely be insufficient to change the present trends. Adding new school choice–related metrics to the already onerous accountability requirements is another avenue that, while potentially impactful, must be pursued with caution given what is well known by now about the unintended consequences of accountability.

One option could be to mandate a certain set of school-level activities related to choice and include a school choice compliance score in existing school-level evaluations to make these tasks correlated to larger measures of school performance. Leveraging market pressures might be another way to encourage middle schools to take seriously their responsibility to help students with choice. Many more middle schools in New York City and elsewhere are now competing for students against charter schools, magnet programs, and other traditional public schools. Thus, they might be motivated to invest greater time and energy into working with students on high school choice if the high school assignments of each middle school's graduates were made publicly available on an annual basis. Finally, more ambitious policy changes might be pursued. One possibility would be to implement a weighted lottery that would give priority to historically underrepresented groups in high performing high schools and dismantle some of the long-standing geographic priorities of systems that have effectively reserved spots in some of the most desired schools for residents of the most expensive parts of the city. Finally, many advocates have called for expanding magnet and other programs, like educational option schools that are explicitly designed with integration goals, and these might have the highest potential to reverse the present course.[35]

SIX

When Technology Programs Backfire

How One Laptop per Child Taught Birmingham a "Costly Lesson"

Morgan G. Ames, Mark Warschauer,
and Shelia R. Cotten

The One Laptop per Child (OLPC) program is one of the most ambitious educational reform initiatives the world has ever seen. Announced in 2005, the program developed a low-cost laptop computer called the "XO" and aggressively promoted its plans to put the computer in the hands of hundreds of millions of children across the Global South. Though only two and a half million XO laptops were distributed, the initiative caught the attention of world leaders, influenced developments in the global computer industry, and sparked debate about the best ways to improve the lives of the world's poor. According to the project's leaders, little could stand in the way of a child with an XO computer: the machine would inspire children to "take charge" of their learning, harness creative thinking to become innovators, and ultimately reform their local or national economies.

In 2008, OLPC launched its first major implementation in the United States with the distribution of fifteen thousand XO computers to elementary school students and teachers in Birmingham, Alabama, with the goals of eliminating the digital divide in Birmingham and preparing children to be active participants in the country's information society. Though the Birmingham project is in some ways an outlier within the broader OLPC initiative, which was originally targeted for developing countries, the program adhered to a number of key OLPC principles, and this chapter explores the implications of these principles when they are put into practice. Our findings—which include problems of design, infrastructure, training, support, and breakage—were typical of those reported in other OLPC implementations, so examining how and why the program backfired is thus worthy of close attention. This chapter first discusses how OLPC's laptops were intended to function.[1] It then details how those intentions unraveled in the Birmingham OLPC program. It concludes with lessons for similar laptop programs.

OLPC'S PROMISES OF EDUCATIONAL REVOLUTION

The vision behind the One Laptop per Child project was shaped by two complementary forces: the utopian beliefs of project founder Nicholas Negroponte, founding director of the MIT Media Lab, and the learning philosophy of constructionism developed over some forty years by Seymour Papert, Negroponte's MIT colleague.[2] Negroponte announced One Laptop per Child (formerly the "$100 laptop") in 2005 and remains the public face of the project. His hyperbolic style lent both fame and notoriety to OLPC, as it had for the MIT Media Lab.[3] His unwavering digital utopianism also inflected the project from its earliest days. In both his column for *Wired* magazine (for which he was also a founding investor) and his book *Being Digital*, he discussed complete digitization worldwide not in terms of *if,* but *when*: "Like a force of nature," he asserts, "the digital age cannot be denied or stopped."[4]

While Negroponte served as OLPC's public face, Papert was the project's intellectual father, until a tragic accident took him out of its leadership in 2007.[5] Particularly important were Papert's 1980 book *Mindstorms*, where he describes constructionism in detail and proposes having a computer for every child, and his 1993 book *The Children's Machine*, where he pushes the idea of one computer per child more strongly.[6] Blending Piaget's constructivism (with a *v*) with MIT's computer-centric culture, *constructionism* (with an *ion*) advocates child-driven learning assisted by an "object to think with," such as a computer, which Papert describes as a versatile "Proteus of machines."[7] Papert situates constructionism in opposition to traditional schooling, or "instructionism," which he claims turns children from "yearners" who are naturally curious into "schoolers" incapable of creative thought.[8] He argues that reforming schools is difficult, if not impossible; instead, children should be given the tools to learn on their own, outside of school.[9]

Constructionism's commitment to child-driven learning and its view that teachers are just another (sometimes less adept) member of the learning community were initially taken up by OLPC as a reason to downplay teacher training and other curricular support. "The role of the teacher is to become a co-learner," Papert stated in a 2006 interview for OLPC.[10] In another interview, Negroponte stated his views of teachers more forcefully: "Now when you go to these rural schools, the teacher can be very well meaning, but the teacher might only have a sixth grade education. In some countries, which I'll leave unnamed, as many as one-third of the teachers never show up at school. And some percent show up drunk. So really, if you are going to affect education, you cannot just train teachers and build schools."[11] In the project's later years, these views were challenged by some in OLPC.[12] Nevertheless, they remain important because they influenced the development of OLPC's core principles, which focus on self-directed student learning rather than a strong teacher role, and influenced a number of OLPC projects, including the one considered here in Birmingham.

OLPC's Core Principles

Papert's constructionism and Negroponte's digital utopianism were reflected in OLPC's five core principles: child ownership, low ages, saturation, connection, and free and open source.[13] The first core principle expressed OLPC's recommendation that students own their laptops and are allowed to take them home, which would not only inspire deeper uses but also give kids incentives to care for the machine.[14] In the second core principle, OLPC demonstrated a commitment to reaching young children; its laptop was designed for children aged six to twelve and, due to screen size, keyboard size, and general design, is difficult for adults to use.[15]

OLPC's third and fourth core principles—saturation and connection—were in line with both constructionism and OLPC's interest in radical technologically driven change. If all children have these tools and they can communicate with one another, the organization posited, there can be a massive shift in competencies in only one generation. OLPC equated its XO laptops with vaccines in the kind of rapid, life-altering change they can create, all by themselves—with no need for additional social support.[16] In this principle and elsewhere, OLPC promised a quick fix to endemic problems in educational infrastructure and, ultimately, a shortcut to economic development. Because the organization believed that laptops themselves could create these changes, OLPC's leadership focused only on deploying the XO laptops, not on technical support, curriculum, or training. The fifth core principle reflected OLPC's commitment to using open source software.

LEARNING IN ONE-LAPTOP-PER-CHILD PROGRAMS

Though the five core principles illustrate the motivations of OLPC and demonstrate how both constructionism and digital utopianism have influenced the project, the extent to which these principles are followed has depended on the organizations running each program. Even so, a consistent theme across existing evaluations of One Laptop per Child programs is that they have not lived up to the promise of OLPC's leadership. A study by the Inter-American Development Bank in 2010, for instance, found that Peru's program of over one million laptops was beset by difficulties.[17] Most schools lacked Internet and some even lacked electricity to charge the laptops (which, contrary to popular belief, are not powered by a hand crank). Only 10.5 percent of the teachers reported receiving technical support, and only 7 percent reported receiving pedagogical support. As a result, only 40 percent of teachers who had the laptops at least two months reported using them three or more times a week. Some 43 percent of students did not take their laptops home as OLPC intended them to do, in many cases based on fears that they would be held responsible if anything happened to the laptop. No significant differences were found on national test scores between students who received XOs and a comparable group of students who did not, but students who received the XOs expressed more negative opinions about school and schoolwork on a number of measures.[18] While there are local movements to co-opt the program, there is not yet evidence of any effects in schools.[19]

In Uruguay, over six hundred fifty thousand XOs have been distributed to all primary and secondary students in the country. Uruguay, a much wealthier country than Peru, devoted considerably more funding to the technical and social infrastructure, extending Internet to schools across the country and offering teacher training through in-person, television, and online materials.[20] The program is widely supported by children, parents, and school directors and has provided computer access to many low-income children who previously lacked it.[21] Nevertheless, a national evaluation indicated that the laptops there are lightly used in schools.[22] In addition, in spite of the government devoting considerable resources for XO repair, a total of 27.4 percent of student XOs were unusable in 2010, only a year after most students received them.[23] Using statistical methods that compared test scores throughout the country from 2006 to 2012 to the dates that students received laptops, a team of economists found that the program had no impact on students' mathematics or language arts test scores across the board.[24]

While Peru and Uruguay are an order of magnitude larger than all other OLPC programs, others similar in size to Birmingham's have been examined as well. Of particular interest is a program of ten thousand laptops run by a local NGO in Paraguay, which followed Uruguay's model of more intensive social and technical support than recommended by OLPC, and was deemed one of the best run by several OLPC developers and community members.[25] Despite this support, this project experienced some of the same problems of disuse, breakage, and sustainability found elsewhere.[26]

Learning in Other One-to-One Laptop Programs: A Point of Contrast

The story of other laptop programs, on the other hand, has generally been much more positive. There has been a substantial amount of prior research on educational laptop programs, much of it on "one-to-one" laptop programs, where every student has a computer to use.[27] In most well-supported programs, students use computers frequently, teachers integrate technology into instruction, and programs are popular with both teachers and students, all of which results in greater learner engagement.[28] Students write more, get more feedback on their writing, and improve the quality of their writing.[29] They have greater opportunities to explore topics in depth and to receive individualized instruction.[30] A number of studies report modest positive effects on learners' technological proficiency or academic achievement, while others report no significant impact on academic outcomes.[31] A meta-analysis of experimental and quasi-experimental studies of one-to-one laptop programs found overall positive gains on measurable learning outcomes.[32]

EXAMINING ONE LAPTOP PER CHILD IN BIRMINGHAM

Which of these fates will befall OLPC Birmingham? We see that one-to-one laptop programs are not inherently flawed—they can provide benefits, both academic and more intangible, to students. But is there something about OLPC's model, or the XO laptop's design, that tilts those programs toward failure? To answer these questions, this chapter draws on data from two different studies: (1) a pre-post survey in Birmingham carried out by Cotten, and (2) a multisite case study carried out by Warschauer in Birmingham and two other districts. We first introduce the Birmingham research site and then explain the methodology of the two studies.

The largest deployment of OLPC's XO laptops in the United States to date occurred in Birmingham, Alabama, between 2008 and 2010. The then-mayor of Birmingham, Larry Langford, a contentious figure in Alabama politics, contracted with OLPC to purchase fifteen thousand XO laptops for children in kindergarten through eighth grade (later revised to first through fifth grades) in Birmingham City Schools.[33] Over 95 percent of students in Birmingham schools are African American, and 80 percent of students qualify for free or reduced-price lunch. Mayor Langford stated that he wanted to eliminate the digital divide in Birmingham and to prepare children to be active participants in the country's information society. While these are admirable goals in many respects, an important contextual factor that affected this deployment is that Langford did not consult with the school system to see if it wanted computers, and particularly XO laptops, to be disseminated to its students. Langford also gave the laptops to the children, not to the school system, following principles of the OLPC philosophy. As he stated on the city website, "We need to put a laptop in each child's hands and step back and let them learn about the world and use their brilliant minds to come up with solutions to the world's problems. If we give them these XOs and get out of their way, they'll be teaching us about the world. How many of us have questions about a computer and ask someone who is older how to fix it? None of us! You find the youngest person in the room and they'll have it fixed in a second. These kids get it, and we need to give them the tools that they'll need to succeed."[34] This lack of consultation with the school system and giving ownership to the students rather than the schools resulted in several complications. First, there were substantially more students and teachers in first through eighth grades than purchased laptops. After some back-and-forth, the school system accepted one thousand of the XO laptops in April 2008, which were given to first- through fifth-grade students and teachers at one elementary school about six weeks before school ended for the summer. In August 2008, the school system accepted the remaining fourteen thousand XOs, which were given to first- through fifth-grade students, teachers, and administrators between late August 2008 and March 2009. Teachers were given, on average, two hours of training on the XO laptops during this time. While students owned their laptops, teachers and administrators did not—a point of contention.

To investigate the program, Cotten and colleagues conducted pre- and post-test surveys with fourth- and fifth-grade students in 2008 and 2009. Fourth and fifth graders were chosen for their reading ability and ease of surveying, compared to lower grade levels. The goals of the student survey were to determine changes in technology use levels and types, attitudes toward technology and computing careers, educational and career intentions, and a range of social and psychological outcomes as a result of the XO laptop dissemination.

Cotten conducted the pre-test among 1,583 fourth- and fifth-grade students in 27 Birmingham primary schools and the post-test among 1,261 students in 25 Birmingham primary schools (two declined due to schedule conflicts). We matched 1,202 students from pre- to post-test surveys. Pre-test student surveying occurred just prior to XOs being distributed in each school, while post-test surveying occurred during the last six weeks of the school year after distribution, five to six months after many of the students had received their laptops. The surveys lasted about forty-five minutes and were administered in a group format, where students were read the survey questions by a researcher and responded individually in writing. Research assistants were available to help answer student questions. Here we report descriptive results of this survey that point to broad trends of XO use.[35]

These results are triangulated by a national study of K–12 laptop programs that Warschauer carried out in 2009–2010, focused on programs deploying netbook computers and open tools (meaning both open source software and open educational resources). Research questions focused on the suitability of netbooks and open tools for school laptop programs, the relationship of netbook and open tool use to teaching and learning processes, and the best practices for implementing school laptop programs with netbooks and open tools.

A purposely stratified sample—based on students' ethnicity and socioeconomic status, type of computer use, and model of program implementation—of three districts was chosen for the study: Birmingham City Public Schools in Alabama, Littleton Public Schools in Colorado, and Saugus Union School District in California. Each district was asked to nominate up to two focal schools as representative of the diverse demographic groups. In Birmingham, a principally African American school in a low socioeconomic status (SES) neighborhood, which is demographically representative of the whole school system, was so designated. In both Littleton and Saugus, two schools were designated, one that was principally White and high SES, and one that included large numbers of English language learners and students from low-SES families. Though this paper principally reports on the findings from the Birmingham portion of the study, it also makes reference, for comparative purposes, to the other two districts.

In the two other districts in the study, our research team was welcomed into a wide range of schools and classrooms, and in each we conducted at least twenty-five hours of classroom observation; at least thirty interviews of teachers, students, and staff; a districtwide survey of students and teachers in the laptop program; analysis of test scores;

and analysis of hundreds of student writing samples. In Birmingham, the research was more constricted. District leaders informed us that we could visit and collect data at only one school, as they were uncertain about the degree of implementation at other schools. At this school, we arranged for a two-day visit and asked to observe as many classes as possible during our stay, but we were allowed only to observe three classes on the second day of our visit. These limits on our data collection, while indicative of the state of the Birmingham OLPC program, also represent a limitation of the study. We partially overcome this limitation by triangulating the lesser amount of qualitative data in Birmingham with the pre-post student survey. Data collected included the following:

- **Observations at a focal school.** Over two days, the researcher observed a fifth-grade class, a third-grade class, and a second-grade class, each for forty-five minutes to an hour. Observations took place about nineteen months after the initial laptop distribution at that school. The researcher was free to wander around the classroom, observe what children were doing, talk informally with children and the teacher, and take field notes. The researcher also walked through the school halls, observing the extent to which students were carrying or using XOs throughout the building. We noted that one of the three classes we observed was taught by a consultant from MIT who was using the XO in the classroom rather than the classroom teacher.
- **Interviews.** The researcher conducted interviews with thirteen people associated with the OLPC Birmingham project. Formal interviews of thirty to sixty minutes were conducted with the principal, two fifth-grade teachers, an English as a Second Language (ESL) teacher, the library/media specialist, and two students. Brief interviews were also carried out with the third- and second-grade teachers during or right after

observations. Also interviewed were a staffperson in the Office of the Mayor who managed the OLPC project, a representative of the district instructional technology department, and two representatives of a consulting firm helping the OLPC program at the school and another district school. Interviews focused on the use of XOs and perceived strengths and weaknesses of the XOs and the OLPC program.

- **Artifacts.** The researcher collected a number of publicly available documents about the OLPC program in Alabama since the program's inception, including statements published by the mayor's office and articles about the program published in local newspapers and magazines.

Interviews were recorded and transcribed, and observation and interview data were coded using a bottom-up approach to seek patterns both within and across the three school districts. District and media artifacts were used to triangulate these data.

OLPC BIRMINGHAM'S PROBLEMATIC RESULTS

Across these data sources, we found the OLPC Birmingham project beset by a number of problems, including lack of use, ongoing social and infrastructural issues, and no provisions for sustainability. Collectively, these issues meant that the professed goal of the program—providing a technological means for improving students' learning experiences—ultimately backfired, harming the students it was meant to help.

Low Levels of Interest and Use

The XO laptops and software were promoted by the OLPC organization as specialized tools for "exploring and expressing" that could engage students in "constructing knowledge based upon their personal interests" and "sharing and critiquing those constructions."[36]

We found little evidence from either our classroom observations and interviews or our survey results of how computers are used by children pre– and post–laptop distribution to indicate that these laudatory goals were met.

In fact, the XOs were not being used much at all, and especially not in class. A total of 80.3 percent of the students surveyed indicated that they either never use the XOs at school (20.4 percent) or use them only a little (59.9 percent); only 19.7 percent indicated that they used them a lot at school. And even this low number is likely overstated: though 20.4 percent indicated that they never use the XO *at school*, 29.7 percent indicated that they never use the XO *in class*. In contrast, students averaged two hours per day every day on the computer in class in the other districts we surveyed.

Warschauer's site visit corroborated limited use in schools. While we witnessed XO use in the three classes we were allowed to observe (one of which was taught by an MIT consultant, as noted earlier), we walked extensively throughout the school, passing every classroom several times, and saw virtually no XO use in any of them. Interviewees were unanimous in confirming that the XOs are little used across the district, and press reports in Birmingham noted that, although students said they liked the laptops, use was low in the classroom.[37]

Survey results suggest that the XO applications used most frequently at school, beyond the automated file record system called Journal, are, in order: Chat (a text-based messaging system), Record (which captures pictures, audio, or video), Memorize (for making or playing memorization games), and Write (for word processing). It is unknown to what extent these results represent use inside or outside of class at school, or exactly how these applications are being used.

Interviews and observations from the focal school indicated that when XOs are used, the program most often used was Memorize, which allows students to create digital flash cards. That was also the sole use we observed in two of the three classes we visited. In one class, students opened their textbooks and copied words on one side of electronic flash cards and the words' definitions on the other side, with the majority of students who did not have working laptops with them completing the exercise on index cards instead. In another class we observed, students wrote possessive phrases provided by the teacher on one side and rewrote the same phrase using an apostrophe on the other side.

In the third class we observed, taught by a tech-enthusiast teacher, students used the much more creative Scratch computer programming language. The teacher told us that he usually teaches Scratch only in an afterschool club and that other teachers do not regularly integrate the program in instruction. While the use of Scratch in an afterschool club can be a very positive experience for students who participate, it reaches only a small minority of students.[38]

While classroom use is important to teachers, schools, and the wider educational community as a site to facilitate and assess learning, OLPC did not start out with the goal of supporting such use. What about children's use in their own time? Students with working XOs reported using them about one to two hours per day at home, according to survey results. Some 63 percent of students indicated that they also had access to a computer at home before they got the XO computers. On the post-test survey, 54 percent reported having a computer at home besides their XO that they shared with others, 26.5 percent reported having a computer besides the XO that only they used, and 20 percent reported not having another computer at home besides the XO. On the pre-test survey, 80 percent of students indicated that they had home access to the Internet. In the post-test survey, only 47 percent of students indicated that they were able to access the Internet at home from their XO.

Post-test survey results indicate that over half the students (52 percent) reported using their XO laptop one to two hours per day and 14 percent reported using it three to four hours per day. The amount of time that students spent per day using computers and the Internet increased after they received XOs. However, ownership of an XO did not increase use of computers for academic or content creation purposes. The frequency with which students used a computer to create or listen to podcasts, do research, do homework, create web pages, or share their creations online all decreased slightly from the pre-survey (before XO ownership) to the post-survey (after XO ownership).

Inadequate Social and Technical Infrastructure

The second pattern that emerged across data sources was inadequate social and technical infrastructure. Before XOs were handed out, teachers were offered an average of two hours of paid professional development time to familiarize themselves with the laptop. All the educators we interviewed indicated that this was insufficient, and some also added that teachers showed little enthusiasm to pursue additional (unpaid) professional development in their free time. As one teacher—an educational technology enthusiast who had helped offer professional development workshops—explained to us, "The XO is not really teacher-friendly. It's added to what teachers already have to do, it doesn't function as well as a regular laptop, and it's smaller, and all the other things that come with that, so it takes time to learn. The training they gave us was not adequate, though. I've been trying to provide [supplementary and voluntary] professional development on the XOs, but there hasn't been much turnout. Teachers come to the required days, but unless it was a professional development day when people are required to come they tend not to come." Beyond professional development, other laptop programs appointed teacher mentors in each school who get instructional release time in exchange for assisting other teachers with technology integration and answering their questions. No such system was in place in Birmingham.

In addition to the social infrastructure, the technological infrastructure was found to be seriously lacking. Unlike other one-to-one programs, in which schools own and maintain the laptops, the responsibility for maintaining the hardware and software lay with children and their families, and many were not able to keep them in working condition. Although there was supposedly an XO hotline that parents and students could call with questions about their XO laptops, Cotten found that very few students knew about it. Teachers also reported not knowing what to tell parents and students about how to get their computers repaired. At the time of the post-survey for students, about six months after they received laptops, 70 percent of respondents reported having had problems with their XOs, and 16 percent reported that these problems were not fixed. In each school, some students interrupted the post-survey to ask if we could fix their XOs.

We also witnessed these problems at the focal school we visited, a year and a half after laptops were distributed. In the three classrooms we observed, only twenty-three of fifty-seven students (40 percent) had working laptops with them. Almost all students whose laptops were not present reported that they were broken and no longer functioning, and again, some students asked us if we could repair them. Though efforts were being made at that school and other schools to teach children how to make repairs themselves, at the time of our visit, there was only one full-service repair shop for XOs in Birmingham, established by an enterprising city councilmember who had voted to fund the program in the first place. The school was not an anomaly. Another survey conducted by Cotten and colleagues in fall 2010 found that less than half the fourth- and fifth-grade students across the district still had working XOs.

Lack of wireless Internet access presented another serious infrastructure problem. In December 2009 we were told that less than one-third of the elementary schools in Birmingham had any wireless Internet access at all, and in most cases that extended only from one or two hotspots, such as in the library. Although the focal school reportedly had Internet access in all of its classrooms, one teacher explained that her students would have to walk out to the hallway for sufficient signal strength, so she tended not to use the Internet in activities. In Cotten's post-test in April/May 2009, only 20.7 percent of students indicated that they were able to access the Internet using their XO at school.

Finally, even if both computers and the Internet were functioning, there was a general frustration level among teachers with the XOs and broader infrastructure. During a classroom observation, for example, the lack of external monitor port on the XO meant that the teacher had to hold a student's computer under a document camera to attempt to show the class the student's screen. One teacher explained, "They are slow. They are sluggish. They can't connect to the printers. I don't teach writing with them because I have no way to access students' written work other than walking around the classroom and looking at it. We even tried to set up student email accounts in my class, but the system blocked everything."

Lack of Sustainability

Though the school district was never enthusiastic about the program, imposed as it was from outside with little support, it felt even less obligation to support it after the two men who negotiated the XO purchase, former Mayor Langford and former City Council President John Katopodis, were convicted and imprisoned—Langford for steering county business to particular companies in exchange for bribes, and Katopodis for misappropriation of funds from a charity he had formed called Computer Help for Kids.[39] Though the convictions were not directly related to the OLPC program, they did result in questions in the Birmingham press about Langford's and Katopodis's motivations in initiating it.[40]

In 2010, with a new mayor in office, the Birmingham City Council cut off further funding from the OLPC program as part of broader cuts due to budget deficits. Though XOs remained with students, the school superintendent moved the XO program "to a subordinate position" as he emphasized other uses of technology.[41] In spring 2011, Birmingham City Schools announced that it was moving away from using XO laptops in the schools given the lack of funding from the city council and problems with the reliability of the XOs. Thus, three years after it started, the program met its demise.

LESSONS LEARNED FROM OLPC'S BACKFIRE IN BIRMINGHAM

These findings show that the Birmingham OLPC program backfired in a major way: rather than enabling student-driven learning with laptops, it largely introduced frustration, infrastructural problems, and breakage, and failed to affect student learning in any appreciable way. Though typical of OLPC programs, this stands in marked contrast to well-supported one-to-one programs in the United States, which have shown broadly positive results. Indeed, the two other programs using netbooks and open educational tools that Warschauer observed enjoyed teacher and student satisfaction, improved learning processes, and better student test scores.[42]

What, then, accounts for the low levels of use and unimpressive results of the OLPC laptop program in Birmingham? Analysis of the program suggests that there were three fundamental characteristics of the implementation, all of which correspond to the broader OLPC approach, that differ from other school laptop programs in the country and are closely connected to how badly it backfired: a technocentric approach, child ownership, and the XO computer itself. We next discuss the lessons we can learn in each of these areas.

OLPC Birmingham's Technocentric Approach

The OLPC approach is noted for its *technocentrism*, the notion that the mere provision of technology, outside of a broader social reform effort, will bring about widescale positive educational effects.[43] Birmingham's mayor and city council believed this claim, supplying laptops to children with little funding for Internet access, computer maintenance and repair, or teacher professional development, and without giving the school system time to develop pedagogical plans for them. This is consistent with the overall OLPC approach as articulated by Negroponte and Papert, which emphasizes the transformative effect of the XO itself on children's lives and deemphasizes or opposes pilot programs, formative or summative evaluation, and professional development.[44] In 2011, for example, Negroponte boasted that OLPC would "drop out of a helicopter . . . with tablets into a village where there is no school" and then disappear for a year before returning to see how children have taught themselves to read.[45]

An unrealistic faith in the power of a new technology to bring about fundamental educational transformation, in and of itself, is certainly nothing new. Tyack and Cuban, for example, have documented how similar beliefs in the transformative power of film, radio, and television all failed to actually transform education.[46] Though we are optimistic about the educational potential of computers, we do think it evident that positive changes will require a broad approach in which technology serves curricular and pedagogical ends, rather than a focus on the provision of technology itself. Technology is only a tool, not a magic bullet for larger structural issues in schools and school systems.

Moreover, not only is technology not a magic bullet, its indiscriminate deployment can actually backfire, harming the very students it was meant to help. The problems with a technocentric approach are shown in recent studies on the impact of gaining access to computers and the Internet.[47] Whether at home or at school, physical access to new technology without social or educational support may have more negative than positive results, with the worst outcomes for those already disadvantaged. For example, a study by two economists at Duke University indicates that increases in access to home computers or Internet service providers in North Carolina resulted in lower math and reading test scores for youth in grades five to eight, with African American youth suffering the worst results.[48] An analysis of a computer voucher program for low-income families in Romania also showed significantly lower school grades among those in the program in math,

English, and Romanian.[49] In the classroom, Wenglinsky found that technology use among the technocentric programs he studied resulted in lower test scores in math, science, and reading, with the worst outcomes among students from low-SES families.[50] Wenglinsky and others show that computers have benefits when part of a well-planned educational initiative, but there is little evidence that simply distributing computers to children has much positive effect.

The results in Birmingham are also consistent with what has been found through prior in-depth study of teaching in technology-rich schools. The possibility of benefits depends on the broader ecology of the implementation, including existing norms and teacher beliefs.[51]

The Problems with Child Ownership

For OLPC, the notion of child ownership flows directly from Papert's constructionist view of the laptop as a children's learning machine, and is consistent with the technocentric approach that views children's tinkering with their own digital tools as critical to their educational and technological development. Papert often belittled the idea that children should have to share computers, calling it as unproductive as sharing pencils.[52] He asserted that educational use of digital media would be far more productive when all students had regular access to their own tools. And research backs this: when students have individual and daily access to laptops at schools, they use them for more productive educational purposes than when laptops are shared.[53]

In Birmingham, however, the notion of child ownership backfired when it came into conflict with another of OLPC's principles: one-to-one access. What we witnessed in Birmingham is that when children owned their own laptops and were responsible for maintaining them, the laptops broke down over time, and there was little knowledge or infrastructure in place to repair the specialized machines. This resulted in large numbers of students without working laptops, which in turn meant low laptop use, consistent with other

OLPC programs.[54] In contrast, programs that used XO laptops without child ownership tended to have few breakages and higher rates of use in school.[55] While it is still possible to productively share school computers, a situation in which some students have individually owned computers and other students do not have functioning computers is far from ideal.

The issue of child and family ownership is important to consider beyond the OLPC program itself. That is because educational leaders are beginning to consider *bring-your-own* programs, in which families are responsible for purchasing and maintaining laptop, handheld, or tablet computers that children will then bring to school.[56] These programs seek to leverage extant home resources to support cost-effective use of technology in schools, and we suspect such programs will grow. But as evidenced in Birmingham and other OLPC initiatives, bring-your-own programs can backfire, even in cases where the device is initially purchased for, rather than by, the family. We instead recommend modified bring-your-own programs, in which schools provide devices to children who do not have working computers.

The XO Computer: No Technological Marvel

Though the OLPC implementation approach has been widely criticized, the XO laptop is often still regarded as a groundbreaking technological marvel. Data from Birmingham and elsewhere, however, suggest that the XO laptop was experimental and buggy, and this design contributed to the program's backfiring.[57] Although many of the XO's activities were meant to engage children in using computers and learning computer programming without anxiety and fear, the XO was like other computers in that it could be easily broken, and its relatively low power usage came at the cost of severely limited functionality. Some of its more interesting features, such as mesh networking to connect XOs to one another without a router, never worked in practice and were dropped from product updates.[58]

Especially troubling was the XO laptop's relative inaccessibility to teachers. With a 7.5-inch display and tiny keyboard, the XO was difficult to use for most adults. Though external keyboards could be attached, we never witnessed any teachers doing so. No ports were available for standard external monitors. In addition, the "Sugar" interface on the XO was unintuitive, and Sugar emulation software was technically difficult to install. Thus, teachers did not have a good way to familiarize themselves with the software except on the XOs themselves, something that required a great deal of effort and motivation. This helps explain why OLPC implementations feature less classroom laptop use than other laptop programs, where the hardware and software are more familiar to teachers.[59]

The XOs were inaccessible to teachers in another way as well. It was very difficult for teachers to get access to student work on the XOs other than walking around the classroom and observing it on small screens. In other laptop programs we have investigated, an important benefit was increased exchange of work such as paper drafts between students and teachers.

Of course, OLPC emphasizes what children can accomplish with computers without adult mentoring or assistance, so perhaps the inaccessibility of the hardware and software to adults is not a problem—after all, the XO was designed for children. However, other laptop implementations have chosen hardware and software that is not only suitable for children but also more accessible for adults, with better results for all.[60] Thus, the design of the machine itself—which was experimental, buggy, and ultimately frustrating—contributed to the program backfiring, hurting the students it was meant to help.

AVOIDING BACKFIRE IN ONE-TO-ONE LAPTOP PROGRAMS

OLPC's research and development efforts broke much new ground in the area of low-cost, low-power computing. But OLPC's projects have been plagued by problems stemming from the laptop's design and the program's technocentrist hubris. Far from revolutionizing Birmingham's educational system, closing the digital divide, or enabling students to "come up with solutions to the world's problems," as Mayor Langford hoped, OLPC Birmingham wasted scarce resources on a hard-to-use, easy-to-break laptop that not only did not help students learn better, but decreased education-oriented computer use in the home. As noted by an educational leader we interviewed for this study, "The XO is great as a research project. It has lots of innovative features. But there is a big gap between a great research project and large-scale production, distribution, and implementation in schools."

The Birmingham OLPC project illustrates just how wide that gap is. Though the computers used were the least expensive of any deployed in US laptop programs at the time, at just under $200 each, they did not reap the benefits that other programs have, thus resulting in a high cost-benefit ratio.[61] The children of Birmingham deserve better. And, indeed, they could have had better. If the City had used the same amount of funds for a smaller but better planned program, for example, with individual laptops for all students in fourth and fifth grades, shared laptop carts in second and third grades, and greater funding committed to Internet access, teacher training, and curriculum development, they could have had one of the better elementary school laptop programs in the country, instead of what the local press called a "costly lesson."[62]

What, then, does the Birmingham initiative say about the broader OLPC program? The Birmingham program closely adhered to all of OLPC's core principles, including child ownership, a focus on young ages, and mass distribution of the XO computer. Following the recommendations of OLPC leadership, the program eschewed a lengthy pilot or formal evaluation and devoted few resources to repairs, infrastructure, or professional development. The ways in which this program backfired echo reports from other OLPC deployments around the world.[63]

Our investigation of the Birmingham OLPC program shows that technocentrist approaches are at great risk of backfiring. Any educational reform effort with digital media needs to be grounded in solid curricular and pedagogical foundations, include social and technical support, and involve detailed planning, monitoring, and evaluation. It is also essential that school districts are involved in the conversations and planning; merely having it thrust upon them will not engender success. As schools and municipalities strive to increase access to and use of digital media in schools, they will do well to bear in mind this "costly lesson" from Birmingham.

What Can We Learn from Policy Backfire?

Michael A. Gottfried, Gilberto Q. Conchas,
Odelia Simon, and Cameron Sublett

The focus of this volume has been to illustrate the many ways in which well-intentioned policies in education can and do backfire. Because very little research has highlighted this unfortunate but very real phenomenon, the case studies, examples, and analyses contained in this book represent an important contribution to our collective understanding of backfire, or lack thereof. Ideally the material covered in the preceding chapters will help to improve how policies in education are theorized and practiced. On many occasions school leaders, policy makers, and legislators respond to backfire simply by implementing newer and purportedly "better" policies without first having the frank and illuminating discussions as to why their policy backfired to begin with. In the realm of education, where effectiveness and efficiency are trumpeted buzzwords of the day, this can only be self-defeating. It is well established and accepted that many policies—large or small, national or local—simply fail to produce their desired or intended results. That policies can actually *worsen* a problem is a much more foreign and scary reality—one that this book has labored to showcase. We hope this book will elevate the discussion of backfire beyond the anecdotal musings of policy-interested academics and into the national dialogue between educators, lawmakers, and academics surrounding education policy. At a minimum, however, we hope to help the interested learn not only how to identify backfire in its different forms but also to recognize some of the trends that run through backfiring policies.

While the preceding chapters detailed individual and unique examples of backfire, there were several important common threads throughout each piece. Therefore, in this closing chapter we will summarize the preceding chapters, emphasizing their unique and shared contributions to our understanding of policy backfire in education. We will then provide a discussion of the general lessons to be learned from these chapters as they pertain to education researchers, school leaders, and policy makers. We conclude with a call for extended research into policy backfire in education.

There are two major themes running through the six chapters of this book. The first is the failure to address local circumstance, where the way the policy is integrated within the setting is just as important to success or failure as the policy itself. The second concerns the failure to address agency support systems, where the deficit in communication and inability to address stakeholder issues and support both staff and students within the program are key to the policy's backfire. While there are also secondary trends, as we will discuss later in this chapter, these two themes are the primary causes of backfire in these case studies and must be addressed in order to prevent backfire in the future.

The increased use of standardized test scores as measurements in federal, state, and local accountability policies such as No Child Left Behind has led to widespread use of interventions designed to improve student outcomes. In chapter 1, Shaun M. Dougherty examines the use of such a literacy skills intervention in Hampton County Public Schools' middle schools in Iowa. While the program did have some small positive effects for White, Asian, and Latino students, it backfired badly for Black students. This backfire created an achievement gap that had not previously existed, and the negative effects of creating such a gap cannot be overstated. That a program designed to improve the test scores and later college academic success of its students backfired in this way—increasing inequalities—is ironic at best and tragic at worst.

The local circumstances are crucial to discovering the reasons behind this backfire. Dougherty identifies the attempt to set a districtwide qualification for intervention, rather than determining qualification on an individual school level, as a major factor in this backfire. While using a standardized test score of under the 60th percentile as the districtwide intervention eligibility requirement may have seemed like an unbiased approach, when applied to local circumstances at the school level it *became* biased. At the school level, when the majority of students below that cutoff are of a particular demographic, their identification and eligibility for the intervention can lead to their feeling marginalized, as was often the case for Black students in predominantly White schools. This bias may have long-lasting implications for impacted students, affecting their engagement in school as well as their academic and racial self-image. While district officials identifying percentile as the eligibility requirement may not consider bias an issue, the outcome in Hampton County proves that individual school circumstances must be considered and taken into account when a new policy is implemented.

Lack of or poor communication can also promote backfire. Another reason for the backfire in Hampton County Public Schools may have been the cognitive effects students experienced when told they qualified for the intervention, which was not experienced by students just over the cutoff point. This may have been strongest for students just under the cutoff point, as they received a signal from school officials that they were not performing as well as peers to whom they believe they are performing similarly. Receiving this signal could discourage students from trying, reinforcing beliefs in their own inability to achieve, especially if the program is regarded as punitive. Their lack of effort could influence their attitude toward school overall, and be reflected in their test scores. If school officials communicate both their reasons for the intervention and the logic behind the eligibility requirement, some of this negative effect on academic confidence may be avoided, or at least lessened.

When evaluating backfire we also need to consider how we are analyzing the results. The backfire effects of the Hampton County Public Schools intervention were exclusive to Black students, and while this may say something qualitatively about this policy, this result may also be due to the analysis. The analysis hypothesized that residential segregation would affect how the policy impacted Black students, and thus looked at Black students as one group, and White, Asian, and Latino students as another group. Analyzing each racial group individually, and controlling for variables such as socioeconomic status and sex, may result in a different understanding of the policy and its results. At the very least, it may help policy makers to understand where in the policy design or implementation they went wrong to arrive at this disastrous conclusion.

Widespread state and federal school accountability policies such as No Child Left Behind require aggregate-level conditional status metrics (ACSMs) to hold schools accountable for student achievement. The use of ACSMs relies upon the assumption that scores from tests administered each spring measure the learning attributable to the school and teacher performance and are implemented both to better align educators' behaviors with standards and to provide school/district officials and the marketplace with information on teacher and school impact on student achievement. Chapter 2, by Andrew McEachin and Allison Atteberry, addresses the potential backfire involved in the use of ACSMs to fulfill the reporting purposes of these policies. While the theory behind using ACSMs is sound, McEachin and Atteberry posit that the backfire is due to schools' comparing scores from spring only, without accounting for summer learning rates.

Summer break is a difficult and varied time for student learn-ing, with students from traditionally underserved groups experienc-ing much lower rates of student learning than their advantaged peers. The gaps between advantaged and disadvantaged students grow faster during summer than at any point in the school year, with most so-cioeconomic and racial/ethnic gaps due to summer learning differ-ences rather than differences in the schools themselves. This suggests that comparing only spring-to-spring test results could bias the ACSM results of schools with greater numbers of disadvantaged students downward. The local circumstances of each school—that is, who its students are—can dramatically affect the ACSMs that are reported regardless of school performance. We cannot account for this loss simply by controlling for student demographics, because research sug-gests these demographics account for only some of these differences in summer learning. Holding schools accountable for the learning rates of their students during the summer months inaccurately represents how well schools and teachers actually perform. Furthermore, includ-ing these months suggests schools are responsible not only for their own effectiveness but also for the home lives of the students they en-roll. The unfortunate consequence is that schools with the more dis-advantaged students are classified as "at risk" or failing, even if their school year performance is on par with other nonfailing schools.

The solution McEachin and Atteberry suggest is to determine ACSMs from fall-to-spring, rather than spring-to-spring, scores. By excluding the summer months in this way, schools would account for the different rate of summer learning among students, and the ACSMs would more accurately represent true teacher and school performance and eliminate the assumption that schools should be equally able to raise the current achievement of any student regardless of background. This simple change would allow for policies requiring ACSMs to be kept and fulfilled, while also correcting the unfortunate backfire effect that categorizes so many schools serving disadvan-taged students well as failing or at risk. Making this change in the test scores used and controlling for demographic variables would factor local circumstances into the accountability ratings that schools report. The results would be phenomenal: fewer "failing" schools in low income areas, and in turn fewer school closures leading to the displacement and increased academic difficulty of hundreds of students.

Given that one-third of economically disadvantaged students and students of color drop out of school, many policies attempt to address high school failure and graduation rates. In chapter 3, Martha Abele Mac Iver discusses the implementation of minimum grading policies that transform the grading scale from 0–100 to 50–100, eliminating the lower aspects of the F grade. These policies are intended to provide greater opportunities for students to recover from early failure and pass courses. Though the goal of preventing dropout and intervening to help students turn their performance around is an important and admirable one, the implementation of these policies resulted in backfire, becoming the subject of intense political debate and opposition and failing to meet that goal.

Mac Iver specifically looks at Texas's passing of the minimum grading policy in May 2009. Again, the goals of this policy were admirable: teach students that it's okay to fail and give them second, third, and even fourth chances, and in doing so hopefully increase their likelihood of graduation. The results, however, were very poor. Not only did the policy fail to increase the proportion of graduating students, but by November of that year several districts had filed a lawsuit asserting that the policy infringed on local control. Despite the Texas Teacher Classroom Association's support for the policy, many teachers were furious at their perceived loss of authority. The attempt to avoid divisive public forum discussions by quietly resolving an issue legislatively drove even more public debate at the state level, as the district policies were viewed as a threat to both teacher autonomy and student incentives to work harder. This lack of communication and ideological cohesion prior to the policy's implementation led to disruption and extremely loud dissent. Additionally, because minimum grading policies allowed students to escape the threat of failure, they were viewed by many as schools failing to teach students responsibility—a basic ideological issue that found people on wildly opposing sides.

The lack of ideological discussion and resulting consensus among stakeholders led to much of the political backfire in Texas, and Mac Iver puts forth strategies for avoiding this kind of policy backfire in the future. She proposes differentiating the types of failure and their effects into universal requirements (what everyone needs to function at a basic level in society) and optional skills (for which not everyone can "make the cut"). Mac Iver suggests we view these as qualitatively different types of failure, and thus react differently when students fail at them. If students are failing on universal requirements, schools should be investigating why, especially because this type of failure leads to more discouragement and overall academic failure than does failure at specific optional skills. Finally, while Mac Iver concludes that there is no quick, easy answer to building consensus around the issue of minimum standards (as top-down decrees have not succeeded), she advocates deep discussion and debate, as well as interactive professional development, to change our beliefs about teacher autonomy and building responsibility and motivation in students.

In this age of increasing accountability policies, schools that are classified as failing run the risk of closure. School closure seems like an intuitive way to improve student performance: if a school has consistently failed to meet specified performance metrics, it is forced to shut down. This approach is designed to move students and resources to another school that will better support student learning and enable greater academic success, but does it actually work? In chapter 4, Matthew N. Gaertner, Ben Kirshner, and Kristen M. Pozzoboni tackle this question with their analysis of the closure of Jefferson High School. While clearly catastrophic for the students involved, the Jefferson closure revealed many important lessons about just how policies designed to improve student success can end up impeding it.

School closure has been likened to triage; closing a "failing" school stanches the bleeding, so to speak. Yet, as Gaertner, Kirshner, and Pozzoboni point out, as a theoretical concept school closure received only limited empirical testing before actual schools were closed, students were displaced, and lives were upended. And, in the case of Jefferson—as these authors reveal through both quantitative and qualitative analyses—it backfired. But how?

First, by not taking student voices into consideration, Riverside School District (RSD) officials embittered students and irreparably harmed community morale. RSD's seemingly unilateral action created a climate of distrust that persisted well after Jefferson's closure, when students had integrated into other schools. And to be sure, the upheaval came with a cost: student test scores the year of the closure declined markedly such that many of Jefferson's displaced students lost years' worth of knowledge. Second, students forced into other schools lost the meaningful connections they had with their peers, teachers, mentors, and counselors in the process. The support they previously received from their community was lost. The result was social disintegration and, again, lower test scores and poorer academic outcomes. In all, Jefferson students were, as they put it, "screwed over" by the closure of their school. Years after the closure, Jefferson students performed worse academically, felt more isolated socially, and were more likely to drop out of school and less likely to graduate. School closure, at least for the students who had to change schools, backfired monumentally. And who knows, had district officials used McEachin and Atteberry's suggestion of eliminating summer months from their aggregated accountability ratings, Jefferson may not have been deemed failing at all. The silver lining, or unintended consequence, of closure was that some of the Jefferson students adopted "a resilient stance" in the face of the turmoil and managed to simply "survive" the closure. For them, this was success. For so many others, however, the closure of Jefferson High School irreversibly impeded their academic success—the complete opposite of what the policy was intended to do.

In hindsight, it seems laughable that student voices were not factored in the decision to close down Jefferson. Yet, as Gaertner, Kirshner, and Pozzoboni illustrate, student voices failed to register on any measure of meaning to the RSD officials tasked with making the decision. And this represents one of the key contributions of the chapter: the methods we use to evaluate education policy must be well rounded and not too narrowly focused on the quantifiable. Any analysis of education policy should represent quantitative trends and student voices equally. For the students upended by the closure of Jefferson, this was a hard-learned lesson, a lesson that future policy makers and evaluators must heed lest they risk violating the axiom of "first do no harm" yet again.

The promise of school choice is that the families of underserved and marginalized students will have options. And when it comes to choosing which school to attend, options are good, so the theory goes. Indeed, the notion that options are inherently good is a premise undergirding many free market–based theories. People are rational actors, and rational actors will act in self-interest. Increased options combined with self-interested behavior equates to increased competition in the marketplace. In the context of school choice, this means schools will compete for consumers (i.e., choice-equipped students), and through this competition school quality improves and student performance increases. Assuming the stability of the "options are inherently good" premise, school choice as an education policy appears very appealing prima facie. However, when supposed rational actors are left to navigate a bewilderingly complex system bereft of clear choices, as Carolyn Sattin-Bajaj illustrates in chapter 5, school choice policies—at least as they were practiced in New York City—can backfire.

Utilizing a single case-study design, Sattin-Bajaj collected over two years of ethnographic data from IS 725, a large, historically low performing, high poverty, and ethnically diverse middle school in urban New York City. IS 725 was exactly the kind of school that school choice policies were intended to target—and yet the availability of options was not sufficient for the students and families at this school. In the absence of communication between students and the school as a result of the administration's laser-like focus on accountability benchmarks, school choice at IS 725 ended up backfiring. In other words, the students and parents at IS 725 were given options, but they were unable to act rationally upon them because of the strictures brought on by the school accountability paradigm. In the words of Sattin-Bajaj, "students and parents at IS 725 were left to navigate the vast universe of high school options with minimal school-based support" because "school personnel who were struggling to manage an endless stream of pressures and demands." As a result, the school choice policies ended up "thwart[ing] school integration" and, in the end, "worsening school segregation across New York City and permanent disparities in education access, opportunity, and outcomes across racial/ethnic and income lines." The main driver was the "creation of competitive choice processes playing out on an unequal field in which students with more resources gain entry to the most desirable schools early on . . . thereby virtually ensuring an [un]interrupted journey from elite elementary school to elite high school."

School choice policies have grown steadily in recent years as a policy lever in order in improve student performance and to increase equity in public school systems. But to make choices, people need quality information. In the absence of such information, the students and parents of IS 725 languished. The school choice system is a complex one, even for more advantaged families in New York City. For those unfamiliar with how the system works or how to leverage the system to its maximum benefit, school personnel are supposed to provide the resources to help them make sense of the complexity. But when school personnel are preoccupied, the system does worse than simply fail students and parents: it backfires.

Policy makers and technology advocates have long argued in favor of making instructional technology more widely available to students and teachers, especially among those in marginalized and historically low performing school systems. Often the argument is that increased and effective use of technology in the classroom will inspire these students to enter science, technology, engineering, and mathematics (STEM) fields of study. Proponents also argue that instructional technology will help bridge or mitigate the digital divide. A number of policies have set forth ideas for how to make learning and instructional technology more widely available. The highest profile have been those in which schools or districts make laptop computers or tablets directly available to students for use in the classroom and home, and research has shown that these programs can be effective. However, when mismanaged, such programs—as demonstrated by One Laptop per Child (OLPC) in Birmingham, Alabama—can backfire colossally.

As Morgan G. Ames, Mark Warschauer, and Shelia R. Cotten note in chapter 6, the OLPC program in the Birmingham school system was ambitious and laudable, but there were a number of critical flaws with its execution. The first flaw was that one of OLPC's architects, Birmingham Mayor Larry Langford, never consulted with the school district in advance of its implementation, thereby essentially imposing the program upon unwitting schools in the district. This lack of communication led to low "buy-in" among the schools. There was also a severe lack of support in implementation, with far too little training for the teachers. Unprepared for the steep learning curve, the teachers struggled to master the XO computers and, in the absence of any established support structures, simply elected to not use them. The same was true for the students. Once Langford was arrested for corruption charges the program died out, just three years after it had begun.

Other flaws with the program included the technocentric approach to conceptualizing the OLPC program, the contentious decision to have students own and maintain the computers, and the XO computers themselves. These flaws, combined with the unilateral imposition of the program upon the school district, set in motion what in hindsight seems inevitable: backfire. The intent of the OLPC program was to increase the use of technology in Birmingham City Schools classrooms among its supposedly tech-thirsty students, yet the result was the opposite. Teachers avoided the use of the XO computers altogether, opting for more secure and stable instructional methods. And students essentially did the same; few students reported using the computers regularly for school-related work. As Ames, Warschauer, and Cotten illustrate through both quantitative and qualitative measures, the bungled OLPC program might have actually increased the digital divide instead of meeting its goal of reducing it.

Having examined six very different instances of backfire within education, we must now ask: What are the takeaways? We have identified two core causes of backfire—failure to consider local circumstances, and insufficient agency-support systems. It is vital that we take both into account if we are to avoid backfire in our school policies. Local circumstances must be considered in proper policy implementation: while aspects of a policy may seem to make sense on a broad scale, when applied to the very specific environment of a school they may become illogical. Chapter 1 exemplifies this, as the use of a standardized test percentile as an eligibility factor failed to consider rankings within the school and further isolated Black students. Support systems are also crucial to successful policy implementation, as several chapters clearly demonstrate. In chapter 4, the lack of support systems for students from Jefferson High School after the school was closed led to increased feelings of disengagement and decreased academic success, while in chapter 6 the lack of support and training for teachers in the OLPC policy emphasized how a new policy cannot be effectively implemented without adequate provisions. Chapter 5 illustrates the dilemma of a school choice policy being offered without the accompanying resources to help parents understand how to make decisions about their children's education. Lacking support at the school, teacher, or student level can lead to backfire; if a policy is to be implemented as intended, support must be available.

Yet beyond these two primary issues, what other trends must we consider to prevent backfire? There are three secondary trends that run through these stories of backfire. The first is communication, or lack thereof. Lack of communication between all stakeholders—policy makers, district and school officials, teachers, students, and parents—can greatly increase the level of backfire. Chapter 1 illustrates how not conveying the logic behind an intervention and the method of student identification for the intervention can lead to greater feelings of academic inadequacy and decreased effort on the part of students. Mac Iver's examination of Texas's minimum grading policy and Ames, Warschauer, and Cotten's analysis of Birmingham's OLPC policy show how inadequate discussion and insufficient ideological consensus can lead to discord, lack of teacher buy-in, political backfire, and even lawsuits. Prior to and during policy implementation, communication is key for success.

The second trend that runs through these instances of backfire is the disconnect that often exists between theory and practice. Assuming that a theory is correct and engaging in widespread implementation without prior small-scale testing can have dramatic detrimental results. As chapter 4 shows us, the theoretical idea that closing a failing school will help students seems logical, but closing multiple schools without first ensuring these closures are actually beneficial is overly confident at best and irresponsible at worst. Most teachers realize there is a divide between theory and practice, and greater empirical testing must be the norm prior to widespread change in order to insure against backfire.

This leads to the final trend: methodological errors. Greater empirical testing is necessary prior to widespread implementation, but we must also make sure we are going about this testing in the most responsible way. As McEachin and Atteberry argue in chapter 2, ACSMs in accountability policies are one such example. Again, the theory is a good one, and even the practice seems logical; however, consideration of all the existing literature and data on summer learning rates helps us realize that the method of comparing spring-to-spring test results biases the system against schools serving the most at-risk students. When contriving the implementation methods of new policies, we must consider the existing field of knowledge in order to ensure we are arriving at the correct conclusions. It is possible that had the ACSMs always been contrived from fall-to-spring test scores instead, many schools that were deemed failing and consequently closed may still have been open today.

The trends that we have identified—the failure to consider local circumstances, provide support systems, communicate effectively or at all, weigh theory-to-practice feasibility, and ensure methodological accuracy—are the core causes behind these policy backfires. Yet beyond being more aware of these, how else can policy makers and practitioners work to prevent backfire? The best recommendations we can suggest are reiterated from chapter 1. We cannot overstate the importance of communicating to stakeholders in the community—administrators, teachers, parents, and students—the reasoning behind intervention policies, and school officials need to be aware of how their communities may be interpreting the implementation of these policies. Perhaps most important in determining a policy's actual effects is evaluation. Only through thorough evaluation can we discover how well a policy is performing and what adjustments must be made. Evaluations allow implementers to ensure consistent quality and identify any bias in the program's selection or distribution. Finally, evaluating a policy *concurrently with its deployment* provides the most accurate understanding of where it is going right and where it needs improvement, and allows for real-time analysis and changes.

No policy is undertaken with the intention of doing harm, yet we must consider not just a policy's intention but the probability of its doing harm. Policy failure is unfortunate but not necessarily detrimental, whereas backfire *actively harms students*. We must remember when considering implementing any new policy that student lives matter. Even a backfire lasting only a few years, such as a school closure that may negatively impact only the students who actually switch schools, is too much harm done. We need to move away from the purely quantifiable to realize that there is a qualitative effect on the students who experience backfire that may last years. To disregard that is to go against the mission of education. Educators and lawmakers must embrace that mantra of bioethics—*first, we must do no harm.* A program's harm to a few cannot be outweighed by benefits to many. We also must acknowledge our mistakes and seek to learn from them. When backfire happens—and it will—rather than attempt to sweep it under the rug, we need to examine it to discover where we went wrong, and how we can do better in the future.

NOTES

INTRODUCTION

1. Steven L. West and Keri K. O'Neal, "Project D.A.R.E. Outcome Effectiveness Revisited," *American Journal of Public Health* 94, no. 6 (2004): 1027–1029.

2. Amy Nordrum, "The New D.A.R.E. Program—This One Works," *Scientific American*, September 10, 2014, http://www.scientificamerican.com /article/the-new-d-a-r-e-program-this-one-works/.

3. Susan T. Ennet et al., "How Effective Is Drug Abuse Resistance Education? A Meta-Analysis of Project D.A.R.E. Outcome Evaluations," *American Journal of Public Health* 84, no. 9 (1994): 1394–1401.

4. Richard R. Clayton, Anne M. Cattarello, and Bryan M. Johnstone, "The Effectiveness of Drug Abuse Resistance Education (Project D.A.R.E.): 5-Year Follow-up Results," *American Journal of Preventive Medicine* 25, no. 3 (1996): 307–318.

5. Dennis P. Rosenbaum and Gordon S. Hanson, "Assessing the Effects of School-Based Drug Education: A Six-Year Multilevel Analysis of Project D.A.R.E.," *Journal of Research in Crime & Delinquency* 35, no. 4 (1998): 381–412.

6. David E. Bloom et al., "The Contribution of Population Health and Demographic Change to Economic Growth in China and India," *Journal of Comparative Economics* 38, no. 1 (2010): 17–33.

7. Hongbin Li, Junjian Yi, and Junsen Zhang, "Estimating the Effect of the One-Child Policy on the Sex Ratio Imbalance in China: Identification Based on the Difference-in-Differences," *Demography* 48, no. 4 (2011): 1535–1557.

8. Lixing Li and Xiaoyu Wu, "Gender of Children, Bargaining Power, and Intrahousehold Resource Allocation in China," *Journal of Human Resources* 46, no. 2 (2011): 295–316.

9. Bloom et al., "Contribution"; Therese Hesketh, Li Lu, and Zhu Wei Xing, "The Consequences of Son Preference and Sex-Selective Abortion in

China and Other Asian Countries," *Canadian Medical Association Journal* 183, no. 12 (2011): 1374–1377.

10. Mihai Lucian Pascu, "China's 'One-Child Family' Demographic Policy—Analyzing the Consequences of the Measures Taken to Confine the Demographic Growth of China," *Bulletin of the Transilvania University of Brasov, Series VII: Social Sciences and Law* 4, no. 53 (2011): 103–110.

11. Barbara H. Settles et al., "The One-Child Policy and Its impact on Chinese Families," in *International Handbook of Chinese Families* (New York: Springer, 2013), 627–646.

12. Erwin Bulte, Nico Heerink, and Xiaobo Zhang, "China's One-Child Policy and the 'Mystery of the Missing Women': Ethnic Minorities and Male-Based Sex Ratios," *Oxford Bulletin of Economics and Statistics* 73, no. 1 (2011): 21–39; Hesketh, Lu, and Xing, "Consequences"; Xu Dong Zhou et al., "The Very High Sex Ratio in Rural China: Impact on the Psychosocial Wellbeing of Unmarried Men," *Social Science & Medicine* 73, no. 9 (2011): 1422–1427.

13. Ming Hsuan Lee, "The One-Child Policy and Gender Equality in Education in China: Evidence from Household Data," *Journal of Family and Economic Issues* 33, no. 1 (2012): 41–52.

14. Hesketh, Lu, and Xing, "Consequences."

15. http://www.silverringthing.com/

16. Melina M. Bersamin et al., "Promising to Wait: Virginity Pledges and Adolescent Sexual Behavior," *Journal of Adolescent Health* 36, no. 5 (2005): 428–436; Janet Elise Rosenbaum, "Patient Teenagers? A Comparison of the Sexual Behavior of Virginity Pledgers and Matched Nonpledgers," *Pediatrics* 123, no. 1 (2009): 110–120; Peter S. Bearman and Hannah Brückner, "Promising the Future: Virginity Pledges and First Intercourse," *American Journal of Sociology* 106, no. 4 (2001): 859–912.

17. Rosenbaum, "Patient Teenagers?"; Antoinette M. Landor and Leslie Gordon Simons, "Why Virginity Pledges Succeed or Fail: The Moderating Effect of Religious Commitment Versus Religious Participation," *Journal of Child and Family Studies* 23, no. 6 (2014): 1102–1113.

18. Hannah Brückner and Peter S. Bearman, "After the Promise: The STD Consequences of Adolescent Virginity Pledges," *Journal of Adolescent Health* 36, no. 4 (2005): 271–278.

19. Brückner and Bearman, "After the Promise"; Angela Lipsitz, Paul D. Bishop, and Christine Robinson, "Virginity Pledges: Who Takes Them

and How Well Do They Work?" (poster presented at the 15th Annual Convention of the American Psychological Society, Atlanta, Georgia, May 31, 2003).

20. Doug Elmendorf, "Frequently Asked Questions About CBO's Estimates of the Labor Market Effects of the Affordable Care Act," February 10, 2014, https://www.cbo.gov/publication/45096.

21. Katherine M. Flegal et al., "Prevalence of Obesity and Trends in the Distribution of Body Mass Index Among US Adults, 1999–2010," *Journal of the American Medical Association* 307, no. 5 (2012): 491–497.

22. OECD, "Obesity Update," June 2014, www.oecd.org/els/health-systems /Obesity-Update-2014.pdf.

23. Federal Bureau of Prisons, "Offenses," February 21, 2015, http://www .bop.gov/about/statistics/statistics_inmate_offenses.jsp; Marc Mauer, "The Causes and Consequences of Prison Growth in the United States," *Punishment & Society 3*, no. 1 (2001): 9–20; Cassia Spohn and David Holleran, "The Effect of Imprisonment on Recidivism Rates of Felony Offenders: A Focus on Drug Offenders," *Criminology* 40, no. 2 (2002): 329–358.

24. Melissa S. Kearney et al., *Ten Economic Facts About Crime and Incarceration in the United States* (Washington, DC: The Hamilton Project, 2014).

25. Eric L. Jensen, Jurg Gerber, and Clayton Mosher, "Social Consequences of the War on Drugs: The Legacy of Failed Policy," *Criminal Justice Policy Review* 15, no. 1 (2004): 100–121.

26. Susan L. Ettner et al., "Benefit–Cost in the California Treatment Outcome Project: Does Substance Abuse Treatment 'Pay for Itself'?" *Health Services Research* 41, no. 1 (2006): 192–213.

27. Mauer, "Causes and Consequences"; Lisa D. Moore and Amy Elkavich, "Who's Using and Who's Doing Time: Incarceration, the War on Drugs, and Public Health," *American Journal of Public Health* 98, no. 5 (2008): 782; Spohn and Holleran, "Effect of Imprisonment."

28. Gabriel J. Chin, "Race, the War on Drugs, and the Collateral Consequences of Criminal Conviction," *Journal of Gender, Race & Justice* 6 (2002): 253; Jensen, Gerber, and Mosher, "Social Consequences."

29. Wayne Hall, "What Are the Policy Lessons of National Alcohol Prohibition in the United States, 1920–1933?" *Addiction* 105, no. 7 (2010): 1164–1173; Mark Thornton, "Alcohol Prohibition Was a Failure," Cato Institute Policy Analysis No. 157, July 17, 1991.

30. Daniel Smith, "The Rise and Fall of Prohibition in America," *ESSAI* 5, no. 1 (2007): 34.
31. Thornton, "Alcohol Prohibition."
32. Mark Asbridge and Swarna Weerasinghe, "Homicide in Chicago from 1890 to 1930: Prohibition and Its Impact on Alcohol- and Non-Alcohol-Related Homicides," *Addiction* 104, no. 3 (2009): 355–364; Smith, "Rise and Fall."
33. Asbridge & Weerasinghe, 2009; Smith, 2007.Ibid.
34. Thornton, "Alcohol Prohibition."
35. Donald F. Vitaliano, "Repeal of Prohibition: A Benefit-Cost Analysis," *Contemporary Economic Policy* 33, no. 1 (2015): 44–55.
36. Smith, "Rise and Fall."
37. Hall, "Policy Lessons."
38. Timothy Olewniczak, "Giggle Water on the Mighty Niagara: Rum-Runners, Homebrewers, Redistillers, and the Changing Social Fabric of Drinking Culture During Alcohol Prohibition in Buffalo, NY, 1920–1933," *Pennsylvania History: A Journal of Mid-Atlantic Studies* 78, no. 1 (2011): 33–61.
39. Thornton, "Alcohol Prohibition."
40. Olewniczak, "Giggle Water."
41. Thornton, "Alcohol Prohibition"; Clark Warburton, *The Economic Results of Prohibition* (New York: Columbia University Press, 1932).
42. Thornton, "Alcohol Prohibition"; Warburton, *Economic Results.*
43. Ibid.
44. Thornton, "Alcohol Prohibition."
45. Julien Comte, "'Let the Federal Men Raid': Bootlegging and Prohibition Enforcement in Pittsburgh," *Pennsylvania History: A Journal of Mid-Atlantic Studies* 77, no. 2 (2010): 166–192.
46. http://cmbc.ucsd.edu/Research/student_research/kiribati-copra/
47. Dana M. Bergstrom et al., "Indirect Effects of Invasive Species Removal Devastate World Heritage Island," *Journal of Applied Ecology* 46, no. 1 (2009): 73–81.
48. Philip Bump, "Barack Obama Has Likely Given a $9 Billion Boost to the Gun Industry (At Least)," *Washington Post*, March 11, 2015, http://www.washingtonpost.com/blogs/the-fix/wp/2015/03/11/barack-obama-may-have-been-at-least-a-9-billion-boon-to-the-gun-industry-so-far/.
49. http://www.businessinsider.com/smith-and-wesson-obama-was-good-for-gun-sales-2015-6

CHAPTER ONE

All mistakes or omissions are my own.

1. Daniel H. Bowen, "An Evaluation of the Houston Independent School District's Secondary Reading Initiative: First Year Student Effects" (report brief, Houston Education Research Consortium, Kinder Institute for Urban Research, Rice University, March 2014), http://www .houstonisd.org/cms/lib2/TX01001591/Centricity/Domain/8269/PE _DistrictPrograms/2013%20SRI%20-%20HERC_final.pdf; Kalena Cortes, Joshua Goodman, and Takako Nomi, "Doubling Up: The Long Run Impacts of Remedial Algebra on High School Graduation and College Enrollment" (paper presented at the Association for Education Finance and Policy 37th Annual Conference, Boston, MA, March 2012); Takako Nomi and Elaine Allensworth, "'Double-Dose' Algebra as an Alternative Strategy to Remediation: Effects on Students' Academic Outcomes," *Journal of Research on Educational Effectiveness* 2, no. 2 (2009): 111; Eric Taylor, "Spending More of the School Day in Math Class: Evidence from a Regression Discontinuity in Middle School," *Journal of Public Economics* 117 (2014): 162.

2. Kalena Cortes and Joshua Goodman, "Ability-Tracking, Instructional Time, and Better Pedagogy: The Effect of Double-Dose Algebra on Student Achievement," *American Economic Review* 104, no. 5 (2014); Nomi and Allensworth, "'Double-Dose' Algebra," 111; Taylor, "Spending,"162; Jennifer Jennings and Jonathan Bearak, "State Test Predictability and Teaching to the Test: Evidence from Three States" (paper presented at the Annual Conference of the American Sociological Association, Atlanta, GA, August 2010); Bowen, "Evaluation"; Shaun M. Dougherty, "Bridging the Discontinuity in Adolescent Literacy? Mixed Evidence from a Middle Grades Intervention," *Education Finance and Policy* 10, no. 2 (2015): 157.

3. Richard Balfanz, Lisa Herzog, and Douglas Mac Iver, "Preventing Student Disengagement and Keeping Students on the Graduation Path in Urban Middle-Grades Schools: Early Identification and Effective Interventions," *Educational Psychologist* 42, no. 4 (2007): 223.

4. Christopher Dougherty, "Numeracy, Literacy, and Earnings: Evidence from the National Longitudinal Survey of Youth," *Economics of Education Review* 22, no. 5 (2003): 511; Richard J. Murnane, John B. Willett, and Frank Levy, "The Growing Importance of Cognitive Skills in Wage Determination," *Review of Economics and Statistics* 77, no. 2 (1995): 251–266; Michelle Porche, Stephanie Ross, and Catherine Snow, "From Preschool

to Middle School: The Role of Masculinity in Low-Income Urban Adolescent Boys' Literacy Skills and Academic Achievement," in *Adolescent Boys: Exploring Diverse Cultures of Boyhood*, ed. Niobe Way and Judy Y. Chu (New York: New York University Press, 2004), 338; Sharon Vaughn et al., "Efficacy of Collaborative Strategic Reading with Middle School Students," *American Education Research Journal* 48, no. 4 (2011): 938; Jeanne Wanzek and Sharon Vaughn, "Response to Varying Amounts of Time in Reading Intervention for Students with Low Response to Intervention," *Journal of Learning Disabilities* 41, no. 2 (2008): 126.

5. Alfred Tatum, "Toward a More Anatomically Complete Model of Literacy Instruction: A Focus on African American Male Adolescents and Texts," *Harvard Educational Review* 78, no. 1 (2008): 155; Vaughn et al., "Efficacy," 938.

6. Joshua Goodman, "Flaking Out: Student Absences and Snow Days as Disruptions of Instructional Time" (working paper no. 20221, National Bureau of Economic Research, June 2014); Victor Lavy, "Do Differences in Schools' Instruction Time Explain International Achievement Gaps? Evidence from Developed and Developing Countries" (working paper no. 16227, National Bureau of Economic Research, July 2010); Dave E. Marcotte and Steven W. Hemelt, "Unscheduled School Closings and Student Performance," *Education Finance and Policy* 3, no. 3 (2008): 316; David Sims, "Strategic Responses to School Accountability Measures: It's All in the Timing," *Economics of Education Review* 27, no. 1 (2008): 58; Maria Fitzpatrick, David Grissmer, and Sarah Hastedt, "What a Difference a Day Makes: Estimating Daily Learning Gains During Kindergarten and First Grade Using a Natural Experiment," *Economics of Education Review* 30, no. 2 (2011): 269.

7. Bowen, "Evaluation"; Barb Mazzolini and Samantha Morley, "A Double-Dose of Reading Class at the Middle and High School Levels," *Illinois Reading Council Journal* 34, no. 3 (2006): 9; Catherine Paglin, "Double Dose: Bethel School District's Intensive Reading Program Adds Beefed-Up Instruction for At-Risk Readers from Day One," *Northwest Education* 8, no. 3 (2003): 30; Taylor, "Spending"; Wanzek and Vaughn, "Response," 126.

8. Bowen, "Evaluation"; Cortes and Goodman, "Ability-Tracking"; Mazzolini and Morley, "Double-Dose of Reading Class," 9; Takako Nomi, "'Double-Dose' English as a Strategy for Improving Adolescent Literacy: Total Effect and Mediated Effect Through Classroom Peer Ability

Change," *Social Science Research* 52 (2015): 716; Paglin, "Double Dose," 30; Taylor, "Spending," 162; Shaun Dougherty et al., Middle School Math Acceleration and Equitable Access to 8th Grade Algebra: Evidence from the Wake County Public School System," *Education Evaluation and Policy Analysis*, 37, no. 1S (2015): 80S–101S.

9. Bowen, "Evaluation"; Dougherty, "Bridging," 157.

10. Janice Dole et al., "Moving from the Old to the New: Research on Reading Comprehension Instruction," *Review of Educational Research* 61, no. 2 (1991): 23–264; Meaghan Edmonds et al., "A Synthesis of Reading Interventions and Effects on Reading Comprehension Outcomes for Older Struggling Readers," *Review of Educational Research* 79, no. 1 (2009): 262–300.

11. Steve Graham and Michael Hebert, "Writing to Read: A Meta-Analysis of the Impact of Writing and Writing Instruction on Reading," *Harvard Educational Review* 81, no. 4 (2011): 710; Sharon Vaughn et al., "Efficacy," 938.

12. Guido W. Imbens and Thomas Lemieux, "Regression Discontinuity Designs: A Guide to Practice," *Journal of Econometrics* 142, no. 2 (2008): 615.

13. Derek Neal and Diane Whitmore Schanzenbach, "Left Behind by Design: Proficiency Counts and Test-Based Accountability," *Review of Economics and Statistics* 92, no. 2 (2010): 263.

14. Justine S. Hastings, Thomas J. Kane, and Douglas O. Staiger, "Parental Preferences and School Competition: Evidence from a Public School Choice Program" (working paper no. 11805, National Bureau of Economic Research, November 2005).

15. Justine S. Hastings, Christopher A. Neilson, and Seth D. Zimmerman, "The Effect of School Choice on Intrinsic Motivation and Academic Outcomes" (working paper no. 18324, National Bureau of Economic Research, August 2012).

16. Albert Bandura, "Perceived Self-Efficacy in Cognitive Development and Functioning," *Educational Psychologist* 28, no. 2 (1993): 117; Nicolas Gillet, Robert Vallerand, and Marc-André Lafreniere, "Intrinsic and Extrinsic School Motivation as a Function of Age: The Mediating Role of Autonomy Support," *Social Psychology of Education: An International Journal* 15, no. 1 (2012): 77–95.

17. John P. Papay, Richard J. Murnane, and John B. Willett, "The Consequences of High School Exit Examinations for Low-Performing Urban Students: Evidence from Massachusetts," *Educational Evaluation and Policy Analysis* 32 (2010): 5.

18. Joshua Aronson and Claude Steele, "Stereotypes and the Fragility of Academic Competence, Motivation, and Self-Concept," in *Handbook of Competence and Motivation*, eds. Andrew J. Elliot and Carol S. Dweck (New York: Guilford Press, 2005), 436.

19. George A. Akerlof and Rachel E. Kranton, "Economics and Identity," *Quarterly Journal of Economics*, 115, no. 3 (2000): 715–753; Richard Murphy and Felix Weinhardt, "Top of the Class: The Importance of Ordinal Rank" (working paper no. 4815, CESifo, May 2014).

20. Nomi, "'Double-Dose' English," 716.

21. Bowen, "Evaluation."

22. Cortes and Goodman, "Ability-Tracking"; Taylor, "Spending," 162.

23. Bowen, "Evaluation"; Dougherty, "Bridging," 157.

24. Martin Schlotter, Guido Schwerdt, and Ludger Woessmann, "Econometric Methods for Causal Evaluation of Education Policies and Practices: A Non-Technical Guide," *Education Economics* 19, no. 2 (2011): 109–137.

25. Richard J. Light, Judith D. Singer, and John B. Willett, *By Design: Planning Research on Higher Education* (Cambridge, MA: Harvard University Press, 2009).

CHAPTER 2

The project was supported in part by the Kingsbury Data Award funded by the Kingsbury Center at the NWEA. The research was also supported by the Spencer Foundation, through Grant 201400162.

1. Michael J. Weiss and Henry May, "A Policy Analysis of the Federal Growth Model Pilot Program's Measures of School Performance: The Florida Case," *Education Finance and Policy* 7, no. 1 (2012); Morgan S. Polikoff et al., "The Waive of the Future? School Accountability in the Waiver Era," *Educational Researcher* 43, no. 1 (2014): 45–54.

2. Katharine E. Castellano and Andrew D. Ho, "Contrasting OLS and Quantile Regression Approaches to Student 'Growth' Percentiles," *Journal of Educational and Behavioral Statistcs*, 38, no. 2 (2013): 190–215.

3. Cassandra M. Guarino, Mark D. Reckase, and Jefferey M. Wooldridge, "Can Value-Added Measures of Teacher Performance Be Trusted?" *Education Finance and Policy* 1 (2015): 117–156; Andrew McEachin and Allison Atteberry, "The Impact of Summer Learning Loss on Measures of School Performance" (paper presented at the annual American Educational Research Assocation meeting, Chicago, IL, April 15–17, 2015); Sean F. Reardon and Stephen Raudenbush, "Assumptions

of Value-Added Models for Estimating School Effects," *Education Finance and Policy* 4, no. 4 (2009): 492–519; Petra E. Todd and Kenneth I. Wolpin, "On the Specification and Estimation of the Production Function for Cognitive Achievement," *The Economic Journal*, 113 (2003): F3–F33.

4. Mark Ehlert et al., "Selecting Growth Measures for Use in School Evaluation Systems: Should Proportionality Matter?" *Educational Policy* (Forthcoming): 1–26.

5. Barbara Heyns, *Summer Learning and the Effects of Schooling* (New York: Academic Press, 1978).

6. Karl L. Alexander, Doris R. Entwisle, and Linda S. Olson, "Schools, Achievement, and Inequality: A Seasonal Perspective," *Educational Evaluation and Policy Analysis* 23, no. 2 (2001): 171–191; Allison Atteberry and Andrew McEachin, "School's Out: The Role of Summers in Understanding Achievement Disparities" (paper presented at the annual Society for Research on Educational Effectiveness conference, Washington, DC, March 5–7, 2015); Douglas B. Downey, Paul T. Von Hippel, and Beckett A. Broh, "Are Schools the Great Equalizer? Cognitive Inequality During the Summer Months and the School Year," *American Sociological Review* 69, no. 5 (2004): 613–635; Seth Gershenson and Michael Hayes, "The Implications of Summer Learning Loss for Value-Added Estimates of Teacher Effectiveness" (paper presented at the Association for Education Finance and Policy conference, San Antonio, TX, March 13–15, 2014).

7. Bengt Holmstrom and Paul Milgrom, "Multitask Principal-Agent Analyses: Incentive Contracts, Asset Ownership, and Job Design," *Journal of Law, Economics, & Organization* 7 (1991): 24–52; Candice Prendergast, "The Provision of Incentives in Firms," *Journal of Economic Literature* 37, no. 1 (1999): 7–63; Marshall S. Smith and Jennifer A. O'Day, "Systemic School Reform," in *The Politics of Curriculum and Testing*, eds. Susan. H. Fuhrman and Betty Malen (New York: Falmer Press, 1990), 233–267.

8. Étienne Charbonneau and Gregg G. Van Ryzin, "Performance Measures and Parental Satisfaction with New York City Schools," *American Review of Public Administration* 42, no. 1 (2011): 54–65; David N. Figlio and Susanna Loeb, "School Accountability," in *Handbooks in Economics: Economics of Education*, vol. 3, eds. Eric A. Hanushek, Stephin. J. Machin, and Ludger Woessmann (North-Holland, The Netherlands: Elsevier, 2011), 383–421.

9. Raj Chetty, John N. Friedman, and Jonah E. Rockoff, "Measuring the Impacts of Teachers II: Teacher Value-Added and Student Outcomes in Adulthood," *American Economic Review* 104, no. 9 (2014): 2633–2679.

10. Polikoff et al., "The Waive of the Future?"

11. Figlio and Loeb, "School Accountability."

12. Robert Balfanz et al., "Are NCLB's Measures, Incentives, and Improvement Strategies the Right Ones for the Nation's Low-Performing High Schools?" *American Educational Research Journal* 44, no. 3 (2007): 559–593; Donald Boyd et al., "The Impact of Assessment and Accountability on Teacher Recruitment and Retention: Are There Unintended Consequences?" *Public Finance Review* 36, no. 1 (2008): 88–111.

13. Mark Ehlert et al., "The Sensitivity of Value-Added Estimates to Specification Adjustments: Evidence from School- and Teacher-Level Models in Missouri," *Statistics and Public Policy* 1, no. 1 (2013): 19–27; Daniel Goldhaber and Michael Hansen, "Is It Just a Bad Class? Assessing the Long-Term Stability of Estimated Teacher Performance," *Economica* 80, no. 319 (2013): 589–612; Daniel F. McCaffrey et al., "The Intertemporal Variability of Teacher Effect Estimates," *Education Finance and Policy* 4, no. 4 (2009): 572–606; John Papay, "Different Tests, Different Answers: The Stability of Teacher Value-Added Estimates Across Outcome Measures," *American Educational Research Journal* 48 (2011): 163–193.

14. Gershenson and Hayes, "Implications of Summer Learning Loss"; Papay, "Different Tests, Different Answers"; Downey, Von Hippel, and Broh, "Are Schools the Great Equalizer?"

15. Polikoff et al., "The Waive of the Future?"

16. Harris Cooper et al., "The Effects of Summer Vacation on Achievement Test Scores: A Narrative and Meta-Analytic Review," *Review of Educational Research* 66, no. 3 (1996): 227–268; Downey, Von Hippel, and Broh, "Are Schools the Great Equalizer?"; Heyns, *Summer Learning*.

17. Seth Gershenson, "Do Summer Time-Use Gaps Vary by Socioeconomic Status?" *American Educational Research Journal* 50, no. 6 (2013): 1219–1248.

18. See the discussion in McEachin and Atteberry, "Impact of Summer Learning Loss."

19. Downey, Von Hippel, and Broh, "Are Schools the Great Equalizer?"; Gershenson and Hayes, "Implications of Summer Learning Loss"; Papay, "Different Tests, Different Answers"; McEachin and Atteberry, "Impact of Summer Learning Loss."

20. See McEachin and Atteberry, "Impact of Summer Learning Loss," for a related analysis of students' summer learning loss and school value -added models.

21. We do not standardize students' reading or math MAP scores because the scores are on a vertical and interval scale, and are normally distributed.

22. For more information about the data, see McEachin and Atteberry, "Impact of Summer Learning Loss," or Atteberry and McEachin, "School's Out."

23. Damien W. Betenbenner, *A Technical Overview of Student Growth Percentile Methodology: Student Growth Percentiles and Percentile Growth Projections/Trajectories* (Dover, NH: National Center for the Improvement of Educational Assessment, 2011).

24. For example, Guarino, Reckase, and Wooldridge ("Value-Added Measures") find that SGPs do less well than other ACMSs in reproducing true teacher effects when students are under nonrandom assignment.

25. Gershenson and Hayes, "Implications of Summer Learning Loss"; Papay, "Different Tests, Different Answers."

26. David N. Figlio and Lawence W. Kenny, "Public Sector Performance Measurement and Stakeholder Support," *Journal of Public Economics* 93, nos. 9 and 10 (2009): 1069–1077; Rebecca Jacobsen, Andrew Saultz, and Jefferey W. Snyder, "When Accountability Strategies Collide: Do Policy Changes That Raise Accountability Standards Also Erode Public Satisfaction?" *Educational Policy* 27, no. 2 (2013): 360–389.

27. Castellano and Ho, "Constrasting OLS and Quantile Regression Approaches"; Ehlert et al., "Selecting Growth Measures"; Cassandra M. Guarino et al., "A Comparison of Growth Percentile and Value-Added Models of Teacher Performance," *Statistics and Public Policy* 2 (2015).

28. See McEachin and Atteberry, "Impact of Summer Learning Loss," for more detail.

29. Ehlert et al., "Selecting Growth Measures"; Guarino, Reckase, and Wooldridge, "Value-Added Measures."

CHAPTER 3

1. Robert Balfanz and Nettie Legters, Locating the Dropout Crisis. Which High Schools Produce the Nation's Dropouts? Where Are They Located? Who Attends Them? Report 70 (Baltimore: Johns Hopkins University Center for Research on Students Placed at Risk, 2004), http://

eric.ed.gov/?id=ED484525; Robert Balfanz and Nettie Legters, "Closing 'Dropout Factories': The Graduation-Rate Crisis We Know, and What Can Be Done About It," Education Week, June 11, 2006, http://www .edweek.org/ew/articles/2006/07/12/42balfanz.h25.html.

2. See Elaine Allensworth and John Easton, *What Matters for Staying On-Track and Graduating in Chicago Public High Schools* (Chicago: Consortium on Chicago School Research, 2007); Robert Balfanz, Liza Herzog, and Douglas Mac Iver, "Preventing Student Disengagement and Keeping Students on the Graduation Path in Urban Middle-Grades Schools: Early Identification and Effective Interventions," *Educational Psychologist* 42, no. 4 (2007): 223–235; Martha Mac Iver and Matthew Messel, "The ABCs of Keeping on Track to Graduation: Research Findings from Baltimore," *Journal of Education for Students Placed at Risk* 18, no. 1 (2013): 50–67.

3. See Thomas R. Guskey, "Computerized Gradebooks and the Myth of Objectivity," *Phi Delta Kappan* 83, no. 10 (2002): 775–780; Douglas B. Reeves, "The Case Against the Zero," *Phi Delta Kappan* 86, no. 4 (2004): 324–325.

4. Theodore Carey and James Carifo, "The Minimum Grading Controversy: Results of a Quantitative Study of Seven Years of Grading Data from an Urban High School," *Educational Researcher* 41, no. 6 (2012): 201–208; Theodore Carey and James Carifo, "A Critical Examination of Current Minimum Grading Policy Recommendations," *High School Journal* 93, no. 1 (2009): 23–37; James Carifo and Theodore Carey, "Do Minimum Grading Practices Lower Academic Standards and Produce Social Promotions?" *Educational Horizons* 88, no. 2 (2010): 219–230.

5. Steve Friess, "At Some Schools, Failure Goes from Zero to 50," *USA Today*, May 18, 2008, http://usatoday30.usatoday.com/news/education /2008-05-18-zeroes-main_N.htm.

6. National Association of Secondary School Principals, "Principal's Update 5/20/08," http://www.principals.org/Content.aspx?topic=57561.

7. Christopher Paslay, "Phila School District Must Drop Minimum-50 Grading Policy," *Chalk & Talk: Perspectives on Education by Philadelphia Public School Teachers* (blog), October 20, 2008, https://chalkandtalk .wordpress.com/2008/10/20/phila-school-district-must-drop-minimum -50-grading-policy/.

8. Texas Classroom Teachers Association, "Major Issues of the 81st Legislative Session and TCTA's Accomplishments," https://tcta.org/node

/11382-major_issues_of_the_81st_legislative _session_and_tctas
_accomplishments.

9. Senate of Texas, Office of Senator Jane Nelson, "Senate Panel Endorses
Truth-in-Grading Legislation," news release, April 14, 2009, http://
www.nelson.senate.state.tx.us/pr09/p041409a.htm.

10. Senate of Texas, Office of Senator Jane Nelson, "Counting Down to Ad-
journment: Bill Status Report," June 1, 2009, http://www.nelson.senate
.state.tx.us/pr09/p060109a.htm.

11. "S. B. No. 2033," http://www.legis.state.tx.us/tlodocs/81R/billtext/pdf
/SB02033F.pdf. Also see "Killing Minimum Grades in Texas," Education
Week Teacher WebWatch (blog), April 13, 2009, http://blogs.edweek.org
/teachers/webwatch/2009/04/killing_minimum_grades_in_texa.html.

12. Texas Education Agency, "TEA Correspondence," October 16, 2009,
http://ritter.tea.state.tx.us/taa/comm101609.html.

13. Mary Alys Cherry, "CCISD Joins in Grading Lawsuit," *The Citizen*, November 22, 2010, http://www.yourhoustonnews.com/bay_area/news
/ccisd-joins-in-grading-lawsuit/article_46579805-a950-5c34-b568
-64b355e36118.html?mode=jqm.

14. Senate of Texas, Office of Senator Jane Nelson. "Senator Nelson Criti-
cizes School Districts' Lawsuit Over Truth-in-Grading Law." November 19, 2009, http://www.nelson.senate.state.tx.us/pr09/p112409a.htm.
Also see "Senator Nelson: School District Grading Policy Lawsuit 'Misguided,'" posted November 24, 2009, http://senatorjanenelson.blogspot
.com/2009/11/senator-nelson-school-district-grading.html.

15. Texas Classroom Teacher Association, "How a Bill Became a Law . . . and
Was Ignored," https://tcta.org/node/11603-how_a_bill_became_a_law
_and_was_ignored.

16. Texas AFT, "As School Year Starts, Teachers' Grading Authority Bolstered," Texas AFT, August 24, 2010, http://www.texasaft.org/as-school
-year-starts-teachers-grading-authority-bolstered.

17. Senate of Texas, Office of Senator Jane Nelson, "House Public Education
Passes Truth-in-Grading Bill," news release, May 3, 2011, http://www
.nelson.senate.state.tx.us/pr11/p050311a.htm.

18. Dorothea Weir, *The Dallas ISD On-Track Indicator, 2013–14* (Dallas: Dallas Independent School District, 2014), http://dallasisd.org/Page/31861.

19. Susan Austin and Richard McCann, "Here's Another Arbitrary Grade
for Your Collection: A Statewide Study of Grading Policies" (paper presented at the annual meeting of the American Educational Research

Association, San Francisco, April 20–24, 2002); Judith Warren Little, "The Persistence of Privacy: Autonomy and Initiative in Teachers' Professional Relations," *Teachers College Record* 91, no. 4 (1990): 509–536; Daniel L. Kain, "Looking Beneath the Surface: Teacher Collaboration through the Lens of Grading Practices," *Teachers College Press* 97, no. 4 (1996): 569. Also see James H. McMillan, "Secondary Teachers Classroom Assessment and Grading Practices," *Educational Measurement: Issues and Practice*, 20, no. 1 (2001): 20–32.

20. Keni Brayton Cox, "Putting Classroom Grading on the Table: A Reform in Progress," *American Secondary Education* 40, no. 1 (2011): 67–68.

21. Pamela Kripke, "Anatomy of a Grievance: Being Asked to Change Students' Grades," *Huffington Post*, April 7, 2011, http://www.huffingtonpost.com/pamela-kripke/changing-students-grades_b_844804.html.

22. Ohio School Boards Association, "First Amendment: Retaliation: District Court Denies School District's Request for Summary Judgment after Administrator Directed Staff Not to Follow Board-Approved Grading Scale," http://www.ohioschoolboards.org/school-law-summary-2012-3-and-2012-4-5#SLS12-3o. Also see "Goudeau v. East Baton Rouge Parish School Board," civil action no. 10-303-FJP-SCR, 951 F.Supp.2d 874 (2012), http://www.leagle.com/decision/In%20Adv%20FDCO%20140313-000106.

23. "School District's New Grading Policy: No Scores Lower Than 60 Percent," Fox News Insider Blog, January 24, 2015, http://insider.foxnews.com/2015/01/24/school-districts-new-grading-policy-students-cant-score-lower-60-percent.

24. Books like the following are highly popular, especially in the business world: Tim Harford, *Adapt: Why Success Always Starts with Failure* (New York: Farrar, Straus and Giroux, 2011); Ralph Heath, *Celebrating Failure: The Power of Taking Risks, Making Mistakes, and Thinking Big* (Pompton Plains, NJ: The Career Press, 2009); Charles C. Manz, *The Power of Failure: 27 Ways to Turn Life's Setbacks into Success* (San Francisco: Berrett-Koehler Publishers, 2002); John C. Maxwell, *Failing Forward: Turning Mistakes into Stepping Stones for Success* (Nashville: Thomas Nelson, 2007).

25. "An A–Z of Business Quotations: Failure," the *Economist*'s Schumpeter blog, July 27, 2012, http://www.economist.com/blogs/schumpeter/2012/07/z-business-quotations-2.

26. Marc Smith, "Importance of Failure: Why Olympians and A-Level Students All Need to Fail," the *Guardian*'s Teacher Network blog, August 16, 2012, http://www.guardian.co.uk/teacher-network/2012/aug/16/a-level-student-success-failure; Paul Tough, "What If the Secret to Success Is Failure?" *New York Times Magazine*, September 14, 2011, http://www.nytimes.com/2011/09/18/magazine/what-if-the-secret-to-success-is-failure.html.

27. Paul Cancellieri, "Why Minimum Grades Are Lies," Scripted Spontaneity (blog), April 17, 2014, http://www.scriptedspontaneity.com/2014/04/why-minimum-grades-are-lies/.

28. Dorothea Anagnostopoulos and Stacey Rutledge, "Making Sense of School Sanctioning Policies in Urban High Schools," *Teachers College Record* 109, no. 5 (2007): 1284; also see Dorothea Anagnostopoulos, "The New Accountability, Student Failure, and Teachers' Work in Urban High Schools," *Educational Policy* 17, no. 3 (2003): 291–316.

29. Allensworth and Easton, *What Matters*.

30. See, for example, Diane S. Kaplan, B. Mitchell Peck, and Howard B. Kaplan, "Decomposing the Academic Failure-Dropout Relationship: A Longitudinal Analysis," *Journal of Educational Research* 90, no. 6 (1997): 331–343.

31. James H. Eck et al., "Noteworthy Perspectives: High Reliability Organizations in Education," Denver: McREL, 2011: 21, http://www.mcrel.org/products-and-services/products/product-listing/01_99/product-87.

32. Valerie Lee and Julia B. Smith, "Collective Responsibility for Learning and Its Effects on Gains in Achievement for Early Secondary Students," *American Journal of Education* 104, no. 2 (1996): 103–147.

CHAPTER 4

1. For further methodological detail on the qualitative analytic procedures that underlie these analyses, readers should consult Ben Kirshner and Kristen Pozzoboni, "Student Interpretations of a School Closure: Implications for Student Voice in Equity-Based School Reform," *Teachers College Record* 113, no. 8 (2011): 1633–1667, and Ben Kirshner, Matthew Gaertner, and Kristen Pozzoboni, "Tracing Transitions: The Effect of High School Closure on Displaced Students," *Educational Evaluation and Policy Analysis* 32, no. 3 (2010): 407–429. For further detail on the statistical models that underlie the quantitative component, readers should consult Kirshner, Gaertner, and Pozzoboni, "Tracing Transitions."

2. RSD agreed that it would be important to track Jefferson students' experiences through the closure and the subsequent transition, and after receiving assurances that the study would draw upon and represent the full range of students' experiences, RSD became a partner in the research effort.

3. These are common conditions when schools are closed; closure decisions tend to impact low-income students of color attending schools with fewer college prep courses, less qualified teachers, and generally weaker instruction. See, for example, Prudence Carter and Kevin Welner, *Closing the Opportunity Gap* (New York: Oxford University Press, 2013) and Linda Darling-Hammond, "Inequality and the Right to Learn: Access to Qualified Teachers in California's Public Schools," *Teachers College Record* 106, no. 10 (2004): 1936–1966.

4. Concerns about students' academic prospects in struggling urban schools are not unwarranted. Some estimates suggest only 52 percent of students in America's largest cities graduate high school. See Christopher Swanson, *Cities in Crisis 2008: A Special Analytic Report on High School Graduation* (Bethesda, MD: Editorial Projects in Education Research Center, 2008).

5. Jefferson did reopen after a year, to a new cohort of ninth-grade students in 2007–2008. Although those students' experiences and academic progress relative to their Jefferson predecessors is an important topic for future research, this chapter's focus is on the students displaced by the closure.

6. For the achievement analysis, statewide tests were vertically scaled—that is, placed on a score scale that spans multiple grade levels.

7. Districtwide growth patterns for RSD students fitting the same demographic profile were similar, although their yearly gains in math (14 points) and reading (11) were smaller.

8. See Kirshner, Gaertner, and Pozzoboni, "Tracing Transitions," for the multilevel model specifications used estimate Jefferson and RSD students' score trends.

9. Pauline Lipman and Alecia Person, *Students as Collateral Damage? A Preliminary Study of the Renaissance 2010 School Closings in the Midsouth* (Chicago: Kenwood Oakland Community Organization, 2007).

10. "Typical score growth" is defined here as the average growth that would be expected for displaced students, based on the comparison group: historic Jefferson students who were (1) Black or Latino, and (2) eligible for FRPL.

11. "Typical score growth" is defined here as the average growth that would be expected for displaced students, based on the comparison group: other RSD students who were (1) Black or Latino, and (2) eligible for FRPL.

12. Figure 4.1 is a "prototypical plot," based on fixed-effects estimates from a multilevel model of test score change over time (Kirshner, Gaertner, and Pozzoboni, "Tracing Transitions"). In figure 4.1, historic Jefferson students are grouped with displaced students prior to the closure, because before the closure, displaced students' scores and score trends were quite similar to those of their historical counterparts.

13. Marisa de la Torre and Julia Gwynne, *When Schools Close: Effects on Displaced Students in Chicago Public Schools* (Chicago: Consortium on Chicago School Research, 2009).

14. The dropout analysis also required a "nested dichotomies" modification to the standard binary logistic regression model. Our data were longitudinal, so a student's presence in one year was strictly dependent upon whether he or she dropped out the prior year. Separate models were estimated for each grade level, and then estimates were aggregated to create omnibus models of dropping out during any high school grade. For further detail see Kirshner, Gaertner, and Pozzoboni, "Tracing Transitions."

15. More specifically, we used principal components analysis to create a standard normal achievement composite for each student, based on test scores in math, reading, and writing. Dropout (and graduation) rates are presented where the achievement composite is fixed at its mean—zero.

16. For example, see Lesli A. Maxwell, "City Districts Tackle Round of School Closings," *Education Week*, March 15, 2006, http://www.edweek.org/ew/articles/2006/03/15/27close.h25.html.

17. For more research on the impacts of No Child Left Behind, see Jaekyung Lee, *Tracking Achievement Gaps and Assessing the Impact of NCLB on the Gaps: An In-Depth Look into National and State Reading and Math Outcome Trends* (Cambridge, MA: The Civil Rights Project, 2006); Jaekyung Lee, "Revisiting the Impact of NCLB High-Stakes School Accountability, Capacity, and Resources," *Educational Evaluation and Policy Analysis* 34, no. 2 (2012): 209–231; and David Hursh, "Assessing No Child Left Behind and the Rise of Neoliberal Education Policies," *American Educational Research Journal* 44, no. 3 (2007): 493–518.

18. For research on Chicago school closures, see De la Torre and Gwynne, *When Schools Close*; for Michigan school closures, see Quentin Brummet,

"The Effect of School Closings on Student Achievement," *Journal of Public Economics* 119 (2014): 108–124; for Ohio school closures, see Deven Carlson and Stéphane Lavertu, *School Closures and Student Achievement: An Analysis of Ohio's Urban District and Charter Schools* (Columbus, OH: Thomas B. Fordham Institute, 2015).

19. School closures continue to be a priority at the highest levels of federal education policy. In 2009, Education Secretary Arne Duncan announced a plan to use $5 billion to "prod local officials to close failing schools and reopen them with new teachers and principals." See Associated Press, "Obama Wants to See 5,000 Failing Schools Close," May 11, 2009, http:// www.nbcnews.com/id/30684025/ns/politics-white_house/t/obama -wants-see-failing-schools-close/#.VSX4zNzF-So.

20. Compare this to Carlson and Lavertu, *School Closures and Student Achievement*, which ignored high school closures and focused instead on grades three through eight.

21. Ben Kirshner and Antwan Jefferson, "Participatory Democracy and Struggling Schools: Making Space for Youth in School Turnarounds," *Teachers College Record* 117, no. 6 (2015): 1–26.

22. For example, see Beth Rubin and Makeba Jones, "Student Action Research: Reaping the Benefits for Students and School Leaders," *National Association of Secondary School Principals Bulletin* 91, no. 4 (2007): 363–378; and Shepherd Zeldin, Linda Camino, and Mathew Calvert, *Toward an Understanding of Youth in Community Governance: Policy Priorities and Research Directions* (Ann Arbor, MI: Society for Research in Child Development, 2003).

23. Russell Rumberger, "The Causes and Consequences of Student Mobility," *The Journal of Negro Education* 72, no. 1 (2003): 6–21.

CHAPTER 5

1. Center for Education Reform, "Charter School Law Rankings & Scorecard," https://www.edreform.com/2014/03/2014-charter-school-law -rankings-scorecard/; Education Commission of the States, "Open Enrollment: 50-State Report," http://mb2.ecs.org/reports/Report.aspx?id=268.

2. For examples of support for the portfolio model, see Paul Hill, Christine Campbell, and Betheny Gross, *Strife and Progress: Portfolio Strategies for Managing Urban Schools* (Washington, DC: Brookings Institution Press, 2012); Michael B. Horn and Meg Evans, "New Schools and Innovative Delivery," in *Blueprint for School System Transformation: A Vision*

for Comprehensive Reform in Milwaukee and Beyond, eds. Frederick M. Hess and Carolyn Sattin-Bajaj (New York: Rowman & Littlefield, 2013), 1–13; Joel I. Klein et al., "How to Fix Our Schools: A Manifesto by Joel Klein, Michelle Rhee, and Other Education Leaders," *Washington Post*, October 10, 2010. For work more critical of portfolio district reforms, see Katrina E. Bulkley, Jeffrey R. Henig, and Henry M. Levin, eds., *Between Public and Private: Politics, Governance, and the New Portfolio Models for Urban School Reform*, (Cambridge, MA: Harvard Education Press, 2010); Kenneth J. Saltman, "Urban School Decentralization and the Growth of 'Portfolio Districts,'" *Great Lakes Center for Education Research and Practice 2010*, http://greatlakescenter.org/docs/Policy_Briefs/Saltman _PortfolioDistricts.pdf.

3. New York City Charter School Center, "Charter School Facts 2014–2015," http://www.nyccharterschools.org/sites/default/files/resources/Facts _General_082214.pdf.

4. Ati' La Abdulkadiroglu, Parag A. Pathak, and Alvin E. Roth, "Practical Market Design: Four Matches, the New York City High School Match," *American Economic Review* 95, no. 2 (2005): 364–367.

5. Sean Corcoran et al., "Limited Unscreened Requirements and Priority Admissions Status: Double Burdens for Disadvantaged Students" (working title; in preparation).

6. John Kucsera and Gary Orfield, "New York State's Extreme School Segregation: Inequality, Inaction and a Damaged Future," *The Civil Rights Project at Harvard University*, March 26, 2014. http://civilrightsproject .ucla.edu/research/k-12-education/integration-and-diversity/ny-norflet -report-placeholder.

7. Jack Buckley and Carolyn Sattin-Bajaj, "Are ELL Students Underrepresented in Charter Schools? Demographic Trends in New York City, 2006–2008," *Journal of School Choice* 5, no.1 (2011): 40–65; Center for Research on Education Outcomes, "Urban Charter School Study Report on 41 Regions" (2015), https://urbancharters.stanford.edu/download /Urban%20Charter%20School%20Study%20Report%20on%2041 %20Regions.pdf.

8. Sean P. Corcoran and Henry M. Levin, "School Choice and Competition in New York City Schools," in *Education Reform in New York City: Ambitious Change in the Nation's Most Complex School System*, eds. Jennifer A. O'Day, Catherine S. Bitter, and Louis M. Gomez (Cambridge, MA: Harvard Education Press, 2011), 199–224.

9. Carolyn Sattin-Bajaj, *Unaccompanied Minors: Immigrant Youth, School Choice, and the Pursuit of Equity* (Cambridge, MA: Harvard Education Press, 2014); Sarah Butler Jessen, "Special Education and School Choice: The Complex Effects of Small Schools, School Choice and Public High School Policy in New York City," *Educational Policy* 27, no. 3 (2013): 427–466.

10. Sean P. Corcoran and Christine Baker-Smith, *Pathways to an Elite Education: Exploring Strategies to Diversify NYC's Specialized High Schools* (New York: The Research Alliance for New York City Schools, New York University, 2015); Al Baker, "Girls Excel in the Classroom but Lag in Entry to Eight Elite Schools in the City," *New York Times*, March 23, 2013; Benjamin Meade et al., *Making the Grade in New York City Schools: Progress Report Grades and Black and Latino Students* (New York: The Metropolitan Center for Urban Education, Steinhardt School of Culture, Education and Human Development, New York University, 2009); Corcoran and Levin, "School Choice"; Lori Nathanson, Sean Corcoran, and Christine Baker-Smith, *High School Choice in NYC: A Report on the School Choices and Placements of Low-Achieving Students* (New York: The Research Alliance for New York City Schools and the Institute for Education and Social Policy, New York University, 2013); Allison Roda and Amy S. Wells, "School Choice Policies and Racial Segregation: Where White Parents' Good Intentions, Anxiety and Privilege Collide," *American Journal of Education* 119, no. 2 (2013): 261–293.

11. New York City Independent Budget Office, "Do a Larger Share of Students Attending the City's Specialized High Schools Live in Neighborhoods with Higher Median Incomes Than Those Attending the City's Other High Schools?," http://ibo.nyc.ny.us/cgi-park2/?p=1016.

12. Elizabeth A. Harris, "Lack of Diversity Persists in Admissions to New York City's Elite High Schools," *New York Times*, March 5, 2015.

13. NAACP Legal Defense and Educational Fund, "Specialized High Schools Complaint," http://www.naacpldf.org/files/case_issue/Specialized %20High%20Schools%20Complaint.pdf.

14. Meade et al., *Making the Grade*; Norman M. Fructer et al., *Is Demography Still Destiny? Neighborhood Demographics and Public High School Students' Readiness for College in New York City* (Providence, RI: Annenberg Institute for School Reform, Brown University, 2012).

15. Carolyn Sattin-Bajaj, "Unaccompanied Minors: How Children of Latin American Immigrants Negotiate High School Choice," *American*

Journal of Education 121, no. 3 (2015): 381–415; Corcoran and Levin, "School Choice."

16. Sattin-Bajaj, *Unaccompanied Minors: Immigrant Youth, School Choice and the Pursuit of Equity.*

17. Clara Hemphill and Kim Nauer, *The New Marketplace: How Small-School Reforms and School Choice Have Shaped New York City's High Schools* (New York: Center for New York City Affairs, the New School, 2009).

18. Starting with the entering ninth-grade class in the fall of 2008, all students in New York State are now required to pass five Regents exams with a score of 65 or better in order to graduate; Sattin-Bajaj, *Unaccompanied Minors: Immigrant Youth, School Choice and the Pursuit of Equity.*

19. Kate Taylor, "Chancellor Carmen Fariña Changes New York City Schools' Course," *New York Times*, February 6, 2015.

20. Milton Friedman, *Capitalism and Freedom* (Chicago: University of Chicago Press, 1962); John E. Chubb and Terry M. Moe, *Politics, Markets, and America's Schools* (Washington, DC: Brookings Institution, 1990).

21. Nathanson, Corcoran, and Baker-Smith, *High School Choice in NYC.* These test results determine students' eligibility for some of the most academically rigorous, "screened" schools.

22. Corcoran and Levin, "School Choice."

23. Meade et al., *Making the Grade.*

24. New York City Department of Education, "Performance and Accountability," http://schools.nyc.gov/Accountability/default.htm.

25. As of the 2014–2015 school year, letter grades were replaced by six measurements: rigorous instruction, supportive environment, collaborative teachers, effective school leadership, strong family-community ties, and trust. State test scores are one of multiple evaluation criteria.

26. Howard S. Bloom and Rebecca Unterman, "Can Small High Schools of Choice Improve Educational Prospects for Disadvantaged Students?" *Journal of Policy Analysis and Management* 33, no. 2 (2014): 290–319.

27. Jennifer Booher-Jennings, "Below the Bubble: 'Educational Triage' and the Texas Accountability System," *American Educational Research Journal* 42, no. 2 (2005): 231–268; David N. Figlio and Lawrence S. Getzler, "Accountability, Ability and Disability: Gaming the System?" in *Improving School Accountability: Advances in Applied Microeconomics, vol. 14* (Bingley, UK: Emerald Group Publishing, 2006), 35–49; Derek Neal and Diane W. Schanzenbach, "Left Behind by Design: Proficiency Counts and Test-Based Accountability," *Review of Economics and Statistics* 92,

no. 2 (2007): 263–283; Thomas J. Kane and Douglas O. Staiger, "Unintended Consequences of Racial Subgroups Rules," in *No Child Left Behind? The Politics and Practice of School Accountability*, eds. Paul E. Peterson and Martin R. West (Washington, DC: The Brookings Institution Press, 2003).

28. Sattin-Bajaj, *Unaccompanied Minors: Immigrant Youth, School Choice and the Pursuit of Equity*.

29. All names, including the school name and number, have been changed to preserve confidentiality.

30. Gary Orfield, John Kucsera, and Genevieve Siegel-Hawley, *E Pluribus . . . Separation: Deepening Double Segregation for More Students* (Los Angeles: Civil Rights Project / Proyecto Derechos Civiles, 2012).

31. Melissa Roderick, "School Transitions and School Dropout," in *Advances in Educational Policy*, ed. Kenneth Wong (Greenwich, CT: JAI, 1994), 135–185.

32. Hemphill and Nauer, *The New Marketplace*.

33. Sattin-Bajaj, *Unaccompanied Minors: Immigrant Youth, School Choice and the Pursuit of Equity*.

34. Paul Teske, Jodi Fitzpatrick, and Gabriel Kaplan, *Opening Doors: Low-Income Parents Search for the Right School* (Seattle: Center on Reinventing Public Education, University of Washington, 2007).

35. For other ideas, see Kucsera and Orfield, "New York State's Extreme Segregation"; Fructer et al., *Is Demography Still Destiny?*; and Sattin-Bajaj, *Unaccompanied Minors: Immigrant Youth, School Choice and the Pursuit of Equity*.

CHAPTER 6

1. This chapter is based on Mark Warschauer, Shelia R. Cotten, and Morgan G. Ames, "One Laptop per Child Birmingham: Case Study of a Radical Experiment," *International Journal of Learning and Media* 3, no. 2 (2011): 61–76.

2. Nicholas Negroponte, *Being Digital* (New York: Vintage Books, 1996); Seymour Papert, *Mindstorms: Children, Computers, and Powerful Ideas* (New York: Basic Books, 1980); Seymour Papert, *The Children's Machine: Rethinking School in the Age of the Computer* (New York: Basic Books, 1993).

3. Robert Hassan, "The MIT Media Lab: Techno Dream Factory or Alienation as a Way of Life?," *Media Culture & Society* 25, no. 87 (2003).

4. Negroponte, *Being Digital*, 229.
5. OLPC staff, "OLPC Mission: Frequently Asked Questions," http://laptop .org/en/vision/mission/faq.shtml#faq5; Morgan G. Ames and Daniela K. Rosner, "From Drills to Laptops: Designing Modern Childhood Imaginaries," *Information, Communication & Society* 17, no. 3 (2014): 357–370.
6. Papert, *Mindstorms*; Papert, *The Children's Machine*.
7. Ames and Rosner, "From Drills to Laptops"; Papert, *The Children's Machine*; Papert, *Mindstorms*, xxi.
8. Papert, *The Children's Machine*, 137.
9. Papert, *The Children's Machine*; Seymour Papert, "Why School Reform Is Impossible," *Journal of the Learning Sciences* 6, no. 4 (1997).
10. Seymour Papert, "Digital Development: How the $100 Laptop Could Change Education," USINFO web chat via OLPC Talks, November 14, 2006, http://iipdigital.usembassy.gov/st/english/texttrans/2006/11 /20061114160233xjsnommis0.2487299.html#axzz3pQIMb5sg.
11. Nicholas Negroponte, "No Lap Un-Topped: The Bottom Up Revolution That Could Redefine Global IT Culture," 2006.
12. Walter Bender et al., *Learning to Change the World: The Social Impact of One Laptop Per Child* (New York: Palgrave Macmillan, 2012).
13. OLPC staff, "Five Core Principles," OLPC wiki, http://wiki.laptop.org /index.php?title=OLPC:Five_principles&oldid=116468.
14. Daniela K. Rosner and Morgan G. Ames, "Designing for Repair? Infrastructures and Materialities of Breakdown" (paper presented at the 17th ACM Conference on Computer-Supported Cooperative Work and Social Computing [CSCW], Baltimore, Maryland, February 15–19, 2014).
15. Mark Warschauer and Morgan G. Ames, "Can One Laptop per Child Save the World's Poor?," *Journal of International Affairs* 64, no. 1 (2010): 33–51.
16. Morgan G. Ames, "Translating Magic: The Charisma of OLPC's XO Laptop in Paraguay," in *Beyond Imported Magic: Essays in Science, Technology, and Society in Latin America*, eds. Eden Medina, Ivan da Costa Marques, and Christina Holmes (Cambridge, MA: MIT Press, 2014), 369–407.
17. Ana Santiago et al., "Experimental Assessment of the Program 'One Laptop Per Child' in Peru," *IDB Education* 5 (July 2010); Julián P. Cristia et al., "Technology and Child Development: Evidence from the One Laptop per Child Program," IZA discussion paper no. 6401, IDB Working Paper Series (March 2012); Anita Say Chan, *Networking Peripheries:*

Technological Futures and the Myth of Digital Universalism (Cambridge, MA: MIT Press, 2014).

18. Warschauer and Ames, "Can One Laptop per Child Save the World's Poor?"
19. Chan, *Networking Peripheries.*
20. Warschauer and Ames, "Can One Laptop per Child Save the World's Poor?"
21. Ana Laura Martínez, Serrana Alonso, and Diego Díaz, *Monitoreo Y Evaluación de Impacto Social Del Plan CEIBAL: Metodología Y Primeros Resultados a Nivel Nacional,* 2009.
22. Ignacio Salamano et al., *Monitoreo Y Evaluación Educativa Del Plan Ceibal,* 2009; Plan Ceibal, *Resultados Del Monitoreo Del Estado Del Parque de Laptops,* 2012.
23. Plan Ceibal, *Síntesis Del Informe de Monitoreo Del Estado Del Parque de XO a Abril de 2010,* 2010; Christoph Derndorfer, "Plan Ceibal Expands New Repair System to Address High XO Breakage Rates," OLPC News, December 7, 2011, http://www.olpcnews.com/countries/uruguay/plan _ceibal_expands_new_repair_system_to_address_high_breakage _rates.html.
24. Gioia de Melo et al., *Profundizando En Los Efectos Del Plan Ceibal,* 2013.
25. Ames, "Translating Magic."
26. Ames, "Translating Magic"; Rosner and Ames, "Designing for Repair?"; Morgan G. Ames, "Learning Consumption: Media, Literacy, and the Legacy of One Laptop per Child," *Information Society* (forthcoming).
27. For reviews see Robert M. Bernard et al., *DMI-ELS ETSB Laptop Research Project: Report on the Grade Three Students* (Montreal: Centre for the Study of Learning and Performance, Concordia University, 2007); William R Penuel, "Implementation and Effects of One-to-One Computing Initiatives: A Research Synthesis," *Journal of Research on Technology in Education* 38, no. 3 (2006): 329–348; Mark Warschauer, *Laptops and Literacy: Learning in the Wireless Classroom* (New York: Teachers College Press, 2006).
28. Michael Russell, Damian Bebell, and Jennifer Higgins, "Laptop Learning: A Comparison of Teaching and Learning in Upper Elementary Classrooms Equipped with Shared Carts of Laptops and Permanent 1:1 Laptops," *Journal of Educational Computing Research* 30, no. 4 (2004): 313–330; Warschauer, *Laptops and Literacy*; David L. Silvernail, *Does Maine's Middle School Laptop Program Improve Learning? A Review of*

Evidence to Date (Portland: Center for Education Policy, Applied Research, & Evaluation, University of Southern Maine, 2005); Mark Warschauer, "Laptops and Literacy: A Multi-Site Case Study," *Pedagogies: An International Journal* 3 (2008): 52–67; Brian Drayton et al., "After Installation: Ubiquitous Computing and High School Science in Three Experienced, High-Technology Schools," *Journal of Technology, Learning, and Assessment* 9, no. 3 (2010).

29. Sharon Jeroski, *Wireless Writing Program (WWP): Peace River North Summary Report on Grade 6 Achievement, 2008*, http://www.prn.bc.ca/wp -content/wwp2008grade6.pdf; Mark Warschauer, "Learning to Write in the Laptop Classroom," *Writing & Pedagogy* 1, no. 1 (2009): 101–12.

30. M. Dunleavy, S. Dexter, and W. F. Heinecke, "What Added Value Does a 1:1 Student to Laptop Ratio Bring to Technology-Supported Teaching and Learning?," *Journal of Computer Assisted Learning* 23, no. 5 (2007): 440–452; Douglas Grimes and Mark Warschauer, "Learning with Laptops: A Multi-Method Case Study," *Journal of Educational Computing Research* 38, no. 3 (2008): 305–332; Deborah L. Lowther et al., *Freedom to Learn Program: Michigan 2005–2006 Evaluation Report* (Memphis: Center for Research in Educational Policy, University of Memphis, 2007), http://www.memphis.edu/crep/pdfs/michighan_freedom_to _learn_laptop_program.pdf.

31. Texas Center for Educational Research, *Evaluation of the Texas Technology Immersion Pilot: Final Outcomes for a Four-Year Study* (Austin: Texas Center for Educational Research, 2009), http://files.eric.ed.gov/fulltext /ED536296.pdf; James Cengiz Gulek and Hakan Demirtas, "Learning With Technology: The Impact of Laptop Use on Student Achievement," *Journal of Technology, Learning, and Assessment* 3, no. 2 (2005); Kurt A. Suhr et al., "Laptops and Fourth-Grade Literacy: Assisting the Jump over the Fourth-Grade Slump," *Journal of Technology, Learning, and Assessment* 9, no. 5 (2010); Bernard et al., *DMI-ELS ETSB Laptop Research Project*.

32. Binbin Zheng and Mark Warschauer, "Teaching and Learning in One-to-One Laptop Environments: A Research Synthesis" (paper presented at the American Educational Research Association annual meeting, San Francisco, CA, April 27–May 1, 2013).

33. Christina Crowe, "A Costly Lesson," *Black & White: Birmingham's City Paper*, November 26, 2009.

34. City of Birmingham, "Education Initiatives, 2 Year Update on the XO Laptop Program in Birmingham," October 2, 2009.

35. For a more detailed report of quantitative findings focused on factors influencing variation in XO use, see Cotten et al. "Using Affordable Technology to Decrease Digital Inequality," *Information, Communication & Society* 14, no. 4 (2011): 424–444.

36. OLPC staff, "OLPC's Vision," http://laptop.org/en/vision/mission /index2.shtml.

37. Crowe, "A Costly Lesson"; Marie Leech, "Most Birmingham Classrooms Not Using XO Laptops Much, but Supporters Urge Not Giving Up on Them," *Birmingham News*, July 25, 2010, http://blog.al.com/spotnews /2010/07/study_shows_majority_of_birmin.html.

38. Kylie Peppler and Yasmin B. Kafai, "From SuperGoo to Scratch: Exploring Creative Digital Media Production in Informal Learning," *Learning, Media and Technology* 32, no. 2 (2007): 149–166.

39. Shaila Dewan, "Birmingham Mayor Convicted on All Counts," *New York Times*, October 28, 2009, http://www.nytimes.com/2009/10/29/us /29birmingham.html; Jimmy DeButts, "Former JeffCo Commissioner Katopodis Convicted of Fraud," *Birmingham Business Journal*, July 1, 2009, http://www.bizjournals.com/birmingham/stories/2009/06/29 /daily23.html.

40. Crowe, "A Costly Lesson."

41. Birmingham News Editorial Board, "It's No Laughing Matter That Birmingham Superintendent Craig Witherspoon Has a Whole Lot on His Hands and a School Board That Doesn't Really Get It," *Birmingham News*, November 22, 2010, http://blog.al.com/birmingham-news -commentary/2010/11/our_view_its_no_laughing_matte_1.html.

42. Mark Warschauer, *Learning in the Cloud: How (and Why) to Transform Schools with Digital Media* (New York: Teachers College Press, 2011).

43. See, for instance, Ames, "Translating Magic"; Ames, "Learning Consumption."

44. See, for instance, Nicholas Negroponte and Walter Bender, "The New $100 Computer," *World Bank Group*, 2007, http://info.worldbank.org /etools/BSPAN/PresentationView.asp?PID=2070&EID=950; Papert, "Digital Development."

45. Wayan Vota, "XO Helicopter Deployments? Nicholas Negroponte Must Be Crazy!," OLPC News, June 29, 2011, http://www.olpcnews.com /people/negroponte/xo_helicopter_deployments_nich.html.

46. David Tyack and Larry Cuban, *Tinkering Toward Utopia: A Century of Public School Reform* (Cambridge, MA: Harvard University Press, 1995).

47. See, for instance, Mark Warschauer and Tina Matuchniak, "New Technology and Digital Worlds: Analyzing Evidence of Equity in Access, Use, and Outcomes," *Review of Research in Education* 34, no. 1 (March 2010): 179–225.

48. Jacob L. Vigdor and Helen F. Ladd, "Scaling the Digital Divide: Home Computer Technology and Student Achievement" (working paper no. 16078, National Bureau of Educational Research, June 2010).

49. Ofer Malamud and Cristian Pop-Eleches, "Home Computer Use and the Development of Human Capital" (working paper no. 15814, National Bureau of Educational Research, March 2010).

50. Harold Wenglinsky, *Using Technology Wisely: The Keys to Success in Schools* (New York: Teachers College Press, 2005).

51. Yong Zhou and Kenneth A Frank, "Factors Affecting Technology Uses in Schools: An Ecological Perspective," *American Educational Research Journal* 40, no. 4 (2003): 807–840; Larry Cuban, H. Kirkpatrick, and C. Peck, "High Access and Low Use of Technologies in High School Classrooms: Explaining an Apparent Paradox," *American Educational Research Journal* 38, no. 4 (2001): 813–834; Mark Windschitl and Kurt Sahl, "Tracing Teachers' Use of Technology in a Laptop Computer School: The Interplay of Teacher Beliefs, Social Dynamics, and Institutional Culture," *American Educational Research Journal* 39, no. 1 (2002): 165–205.

52. See, for instance, Seymour Papert, "Computers in the Classroom: Agents of Change," *Washington Post Education Review*, October 27, 1996.

53. See, for instance, Russell, Bebell, and Higgins, "Laptop Learning."

54. Plan Ceibal, *Síntesis Del Informe de Monitoreo Del Estado Del Parque de XO a Abril de 2010*; Rosner and Ames, "Designing for Repair."

55. Gerald Ardito, "The Shape of Disruption: Student Independence in the 5th Grade Classroom," in *Proceedings of EdMedia: World Conference on Educational Media and Technology 2011*, eds. T. Bastiaens and M. Ebner (Waynesville, NC: Association for the Advancement of Computing in Education, 2011), 2129–2133.

56. Mal Lee and Bernard Ryall, "Financing the Networked School Community: Building Upon the Home Investment," in *Developing a Networked School Community*, eds. Mal Lee and Glenn Finger (Camberwell, Victoria, Australia: ACER Press, 2010), 109–124.

57. Plan Ceibal, *Síntesis Del Informe de Monitoreo Del Estado Del Parque de XO a Abril de 2010*; Warschauer and Ames, "Can One Laptop per Child Save the World's Poor?"; Rosner and Ames, "Designing for Repair."

58. Warschauer and Ames, "Can One Laptop per Child Save the World's Poor?"; Rosner and Ames, "Designing for Repair."

59. Ames, "Translating Magic"; Ames, "Learning Consumption."

60. Warschauer, *Learning in the Cloud*.

61. Warschauer and Ames, "Can One Laptop per Child Save the World's Poor?"

62. Crowe, "A Costly Lesson."

63. Warschauer and Ames, "Can One Laptop per Child Save the World's Poor?"

ABOUT THE EDITORS

Michael A. Gottfried is an associate professor in the Gevirtz Graduate School of Education at the University of California, Santa Barbara. His research examines educational policy and the economics of education. His projects, ranging from early education to high school course taking, have been funded by the National Science Foundation, National Institutes of Health, the University of California, as well as several private foundations. He is coeditor of *Inequality, Power, and School Success* (Routledge, 2015). Gottfried is currently on the editorial board of *Educational Evaluation and Policy Analysis*.

Gilberto Q. Conchas is a professor of educational policy and social context at the University of California, Irvine. He is the author of *The Color of Success* (Teachers College Press, 2006), coauthor of *Small Schools and Urban Youth* (Corwin, 2008), coauthor of *Streetsmart Schoolsmart* (Teachers College Press, 2012), coeditor of *Inequality, Power, and School Success* (Routledge, 2015), and editor of *Cracks in the Schoolyard* (Teachers College Press, 2015). Conchas is currently interim chair of the Department of Chican@ Studies, acting associate dean of social sciences, and visiting professor of sociology at the University of California, Santa Barbara. He has also been a visiting professor at the University of Southern California, San Francisco State University, the University of Washington, the University of Barcelona, and the University of California, Berkeley.

ABOUT THE CONTRIBUTORS

Morgan G. Ames is a research scientist in the Department of Informatics at the University of California, Irvine, and a fellow at Jean Lave's Slow Science Institute. Her research examines the ideological underpinnings of educational technology and STEM education practices in the United States. She is currently working on a book based on her research on the cultural history and outcomes of the One Laptop per Child project. Her dissertation on the topic won the Nathan Maccoby Outstanding Dissertation Award in Stanford University's Department of Communication in 2013.

Allison Atteberry is an assistant professor in the Research and Evaluation Methodology program at the University of Colorado Boulder's School of Education. Her academic interests center on policies and interventions that are intended to help provide effective teachers to the students who need them most. Atteberry has expertise in both econometric and statistical approaches to education policy analysis.

Shelia R. Cotten is a professor in the Department of Media and Information at Michigan State University. She is also the director of the Sparrow/MSU Center for Innovation and Research and the MSU Trifecta Initiative. Her research examines the educational, health, and social impacts of technology use across the life course. She is an editor of *Emerald Studies in Media and Communications*. Her research has been funded by the National Science Foundation and the National Institute on Aging.

Shaun M. Dougherty is an assistant professor of education policy and leadership at the Neag School of Education and an affiliated faculty member in the Department of Public Policy at the University of Connecticut. He holds a doctoral degree in quantitative policy analysis from Harvard University as well as a master's degree in educational administration from Gwynedd Mercy University. His work focuses on applied quantitative analysis of education policies and programs, including career and technical education, with an emphasis on understanding how preK–12 policies and programs impact student outcomes. In particular, he emphasizes how policies and practices affect educational equity related to race, class, gender, and disability. Dougherty is a former high school mathematics teacher and assistant principal. His work has appeared in the *Journal of Research on Educational Effectiveness, Education Evaluation and Policy Analysis*, and *Education Finance and Policy*. In addition, he has conducted policy research for the Center for Education Policy Research at Harvard University, the Massachusetts Department of Elementary and Secondary Schools, and the Thomas B. Fordham Institute.

Matthew N. Gaertner is a senior research scientist in the Center for College & Career Success at Pearson. His methodological interests include multilevel models, categorical data analysis, and item response theory. Substantively, his research focuses on the effects of educational policies and reforms on disadvantaged students' access, persistence, and achievement. Dr. Gaertner's work has been published in *Harvard Law Review, Harvard Educational Review, Educational Evaluation and Policy Analysis, Research in Higher Education*, and *Educational Measurement: Issues and Practice*. He was awarded a Spencer Foundation Dissertation Fellowship and an Association for Institutional Research Dissertation Grant. Dr. Gaertner also received the 2013 and 2011 Charles F. Elton Best Paper Awards from the Association for Institutional Research. He holds a BA from Georgetown University and a PhD in Research and Evaluation Methodology from the University of Colorado Boulder.

Ben Kirshner is an associate professor in the School of Education at the University of Colorado Boulder. His research examines how young people from marginalized communities interpret their sociopolitical context and learn to exercise collective political agency. Ben is co–principal investigator for an international study, led by Roderick Watts and funded by Atlantic Philanthropies, that examines community-based youth organizing as a vehicle for civic engagement in South Africa, Ireland, Northern Ireland, and the United States. He is also a "network advisor" for the MacArthur Foundation's Connected Learning Research Network. His publications discuss youth civic engagement and activism, participatory action research, and urban education policy. He serves as faculty director for the CU Engage: Center for Community-Based Learning and Research.

Martha Abele Mac Iver is an associate professor in the School of Education at Johns Hopkins University and a research scientist at the Center for Social Organization of Schools. After receiving her PhD in political science from the University of Michigan and spending more than a decade conducting research on both the Northern Ireland conflict and the political transformation of Europe after 1989, she has focused her recent research on the effectiveness of numerous school and district educational interventions designed to improve student achievement. She is currently leading two studies funded by the Institute of Education Sciences: a study to develop and evaluate the effectiveness of professional development to equip high school teachers to increase student motivation to successfully earn all required course credits, and a continuous improvement study of family engagement efforts focused on improving student outcomes in the transition to high school.

Andrew McEachin is an associate policy researcher at the RAND Corporation. Prior to joining RAND, he was an assistant professor of educational policy at North Carolina State University, and an IES

Postdoctoral Fellow at the University of Virginia. The unifying goal of his research is to generate rigorous policy-relevant evidence to help educators and policy makers in their efforts to raise student achievement and narrow achievement gaps. His research agenda focuses on the determinants of persistent achievement gaps as well as evaluating the design and effect of popular policy responses to reduce these gaps. Examples of these include standards-based accountability, school choice initiatives, teacher labor markets, and curricular intensification. He received his PhD in education policy and MA in economics from the University of Southern California, and his AB in history from Cornell University.

Kristen M. Pozzoboni is an assistant professor of child and adolescent development in the College of Health and Social Sciences at San Francisco State University. In her research she draws on developmental and learning science to understand features of environments that engage youth and support their social, emotional, and cognitive development. Kristen is co–principal investigator for a study that examines how young people who reside in urban settings make meaning of places and spaces in the outdoors. The study is led by Nina Roberts and funded by the United States Department of Agriculture Forest Service. Dr. Pozzoboni earned her PhD in educational psychology from the University of Colorado Boulder.

Carolyn Sattin-Bajaj is an assistant professor in the Department of Education Leadership, Management and Policy and codirector of the Center for College Readiness at Seton Hall University. Her research focuses on school choice and issues of educational equity and access for Latino, immigrant-origin students and families across the P-20 educational spectrum. Her most recent book is titled *Unaccompanied Minors: Immigrant Youth, School Choice, and the Pursuit of Equity* (Harvard Education Press, 2014).

Odelia Simon is a doctoral student in education policy, leadership, and research methods at the Gevirtz Graduate School of Education at the University of California, Santa Barbara. Her research interests include educational policy as it pertains to human development and early education.

Cameron Sublett is a doctoral student in education policy, leadership, and research methods in the Gevirtz Graduate School of Education at the University of California, Santa Barbara. His research focuses on higher education policy and economics, online learning, and community colleges.

Mark Warschauer is professor and interim dean of the School of Education at the University of California, Irvine. He has carried out a wide range of research on the use of digital media by diverse learners in K–12 schools and colleges. Warschauer is a fellow of the American Educational Research Association and editor-in-chief of the association's newest research journal, *AERA Open*. His books include *Learning in the Cloud: How (and Why) to Transform Schools with Digital Media* (Teachers College Press, 2011) and *Technology and Social Inclusion* (MIT Press, 2004).